D1345952

Sound Change and the History of English

For Elaine

Sound Change and the History of English

JEREMY J. SMITH

OXFORD
UNIVERSITY PRESS

WITHDRAWN

OXFORD

UNIVERSITY PRESS

Great Clarendon Street, Oxford OX2 6DP

Oxford University Press is a department of the University of Oxford.
It furthers the University's objective of excellence in research, scholarship,
and education by publishing worldwide in

Oxford New York

Auckland Cape Town Dar es Salaam Hong Kong Karachi
Kuala Lumpur Madrid Melbourne Mexico City Nairobi
New Delhi Shanghai Taipei Toronto

With offices in

Argentina Austria Brazil Chile Czech Republic France Greece
Guatemala Hungary Italy Japan Poland Portugal Singapore
South Korea Switzerland Thailand Turkey Ukraine Vietnam

Oxford is a registered trade mark of Oxford University Press
in the UK and in certain other countries

Published in the United States
by Oxford University Press Inc., New York

© Jeremy J. Smith 2007

The moral rights of the author have been asserted
Database right Oxford University Press (maker)

First published 2007

All rights reserved. No part of this publication may be reproduced,
stored in a retrieval system, or transmitted, in any form or by any means,
without the prior permission in writing of Oxford University Press,
or as expressly permitted by law, or under terms agreed with the appropriate
reprographics rights organization. Enquiries concerning reproduction
outside the scope of the above should be sent to the Rights Department,
Oxford University Press, at the address above

You must not circulate this book in any other binding or cover
and you must impose the same condition on any acquirer

British Library Cataloguing in Publication Data

Data available

Library of Congress Cataloging in Publication Data

Data available

Typeset by SPI Publisher Services, Pondicherry, India
Printed in Great Britain
on acid-free paper by
Biddles Ltd., King's Lynn, Norfolk

ISBN 978-0-19-929195-3

1 3 5 7 9 10 8 6 4 2

SHORT LOAN COLLECTION
WITHDRAWN

Contents

Preface

It is an interesting fact that students have generally been content to devote themselves to some aspects of the history of English, but not all. Answers are sought to those research questions which begin with 'What...?' or 'When...?' and, rather more rarely, 'Why...?'

There are good reasons for this. Clearly, 'what?' and 'when?' are basic questions; there is no point in asking 'why?' until we are clear about what is being investigated and when it took place. Moreover, as any lawyer is aware, proving motive is notoriously tricky. Refusing to address 'why?'-type questions can therefore be justified on the grounds of an attractive scholarly modesty: is it possible to *prove* that such-and-such an event or development took place when and in the way it did for such-and-such reasons? If it is not possible to prove why something happened when and in the way it did, surely it is mere self-indulgence to attempt to address the question at all. Nevertheless, 'why?' seems a reasonable question for historical linguists to address, and an argument along these lines is put forward explicitly in Chapter 1, and returned to in Chapter 7. The question underlies all the intervening chapters and I hope that readers will engage with it throughout the book.

Some levels of language, of course, are easier to discuss in 'why?' terms than others. With regard to the lexicon, for instance, it seems fairly undeniable that the presence of French-derived vocabulary in English relates to the geographical proximity of the two languages and to historical events (the Norman Conquest, for instance), while most scholars—not of course all—hold that inflectional loss during the transition from Old to Middle English relates in some way to contact developments such as the interaction between English and Norse. Sound change, as has been acknowledged by many scholars, is perhaps a trickier phenomenon to discuss in 'why?' terms. However, this book argues that it is nevertheless possible to develop historically plausible and worthwhile accounts of the changes which have taken place in the history of English sounds, bearing in mind all necessary caveats about the status of such explanations. After all, historians of politics, economics, religion, etc., have all felt able to ask 'why?' questions: Why did the Roman Empire collapse? Why did the Reformation happen? Why did the Jacobites fail? Why did the French Revolution or the First World War take place? Why did the Russian Revolution happen when it did? Why did the Industrial Revolution take place when and where it did? All these questions are considered entirely legitimate in historiography, even if no final, unequivocal, answers are forthcoming. If historical linguistics is a branch of history—and it is an argument of this book that it is—then it seems rather perverse not to allow historical linguists to address 'why?' questions as well.

This book arose from a wish to assess the current status of the 'why?' question with reference to sound change in the history of English. It builds on an approach I began to develop in *An Historical Study of English* (1996), which was a general methodological survey of English historical linguistics. Both seek, but neither pretends, to give a definitive answer to the question. The present book suggests some possible avenues for future work and, along with a synthesis of publications in the field by others, presents some findings of my own research.

The book deals with many of the sound changes which canonically appear in undergraduate and postgraduate courses on the history of the language, but it is not designed as a comprehensive historical phonology of English: there are many admirable books along such lines as well as authoritative studies of particular periods (for details of which, see Suggestions for Further Reading). Rather, I have selected certain key developments in the history of English sounds for thematic reasons and in order to address general arguments. Three major developments are subjected to special scrutiny—Old English Breaking, quantitative changes in the transition from Old to Middle English, and the Great Vowel Shifts. These discussions draw in part on material I have published elsewhere, but in each case the development has been completely reassessed and I have suggested either a new or a much revised approach.

My interest in the 'why?' question arose from questions persistently asked by my students, and the book builds on my responses to those questions. For that reason, though this is a technical book, I have tried to keep the use of technical terms to a minimum, on the principle that 'in a subject such as linguistics, if something can be explained it should be explainable in simple everyday language, which any intelligent person can understand' (Dixon 1991: 3–4). I envisage the primary readership for this book as being advanced undergraduate and postgraduate students, though I hope that their teachers may also find something of value here, if only to dispute. This mixed audience is the main reason why, on occasion, I describe what some may consider rather basic knowledge about the history of English sounds. I hope more advanced scholars will be patient at these points. The nature of its audience also accounts for features of the book such as the appendix on *Principal Sound Changes from proto-Germanic to Early Modern English*, the *Suggestions for Further Reading*, and the *Thematic Index*. It can sometimes be useful, however, to re-examine basic notions from first principles rather than simply accepting current wisdom or theoretical orientation.

There remains the pleasant task of acknowledging the assistance of colleagues and friends who have helped me formulate my ideas and develop the arguments presented here, though I want to emphasize that, in all cases, responsibility for the book is wholly mine. As ever, my primary inspiration has been Michael Samuels, with whom I have discussed at various times many of the issues raised here. Simon Horobin (Oxford) and Merja Stenroos (Stavanger), my colleagues in the Middle English Grammar Project and both at one time based in Glasgow, have been special inspirations and have provided invaluable assistance in developing the argument of the book. My Glasgow colleagues, in particular Christian Kay, Mike MacMahon, and Jane Stuart-Smith, have all helped in different ways, as have many other friends and colleagues in the field from very various traditions of linguistic enquiry. I am particularly conscious of debts to the work and/or comments of Jack Aitken, Michael Benskin, Juliette Blevins, Derek Britton, Alistair Campbell,

Les Collier, Eric Dobson, Heinz Giegerich, Richard Hogg, Paul Johnston, Darya Kavitskaya, Meg Laing, Roger Lass, Caroline Macafee, Angus McIntosh, April McMahon, Robert Millar, Jim Milroy, Donka Minkova, Lynda Mugglestone, Hans Frede Nielsen, Mieko Ogura, Niki Ritt, Jane Roberts, John G. Smith, Robert Stockwell, Ron Waldron, and Keith Williamson, though I am sure that many of these persons will disagree—or would have disagreed—strongly with the approaches and views expressed here. Materials relating to this book have been delivered at various seminars, including talks given at the universities of Aberdeen, Edinburgh, Oxford and Stavanger. I thank the audiences for their comments on all these occasions.

I am grateful to John Davey, who agreed to support the publication of this book and has proven a source of strength and cheerful encouragement, to Peter Kahrel and Chloe Plummer, and to various anonymous reviewers for Oxford University Press. But my primary debts are personal ones, and are reflected in the dedication of this book.

Jeremy J. Smith
Glasgow 2006

List of Figures

Notations and Conventions

For the convenience of readers, abbreviations have been kept to an absolute minimum. However, some notations and conventions are necessary, and these are listed here.

In general, traditional 'philological' notation is adopted. The advantage of this notation is convenience for the reader, since it (a) corresponds to a convenient reference model of Old English orthographic practice, and (b) avoids commitment to a specific phonological or allophonic interpretation (which can be the point at issue). It is also adopted in standard grammars (e.g. Campbell 1959; Hamer 1967; it is also used in Hogg 1992, though obviously that work is much more theoretically sophisticated). However, the standard phonetic and phonological conventions are also used, namely [..] = allophonic/phonetic transcription, /../ = phonemic transcription, <..> = graphemic transcription. For allographic transcriptions, occasionally used in this book, a new convention has been developed: ≪..≫. For descriptive rules, the following conventions are also used:

C   any consonant
V   any vowel
v   'weakened' vowel (see ch. 5)
>   goes to, becomes, is realized as
<   comes from
$ syllable boundary
φ   zero
/   in the environment. Thus: X > Y/A_B stands for 'X becomes Y in the environment of a preceding A and a following B, i.e. AXB becomes AYB'.
*   reconstructed/hypothetical form

I use the term 'Received Pronunciation' to refer to the accent component of Standard Southern British English.

In phonetic/phonological transcriptions, the conventions of the International Phonetic Alphabet (IPA) are followed, in accordance with the principles set out in the *Handbook of the International Phonetic Association* (1999).

1

On Explaining Sound Change

Accounting for sound change has, of course, been one of the chief concerns of historical linguists. By standard theory sound change takes place at the phonological level; as a result, the entire edifice may then be rearranged through new patterning at the morphosyntactic or semantic planes. Yet the assumption of neat strata, with carefully specified directions of interaction, possibly reflects a grasp of language simplified for pedagogical presentation. An unbiased examination of more intimate relationships between the various strata conducive to sound change, with full allowance for an occasional reversal of the accepted sequence or hierarchy, ranks among the key problems of historical linguistics.... (Lehmann and Malkiel 1968: viii)

Speech as noise is only operative socially. One of the first to envisage the problem from the social point of view...was Professor Bally, of Geneva, who wrote in 1913: 'The problem of linguistics in the future will be the experimental study of the social functioning of speech.' (Firth 1964: 173)

1 About this book

1.0 This book is about sound change in the history of English from its divergence from other Germanic varieties until approximately 1800. It seeks to cover and link up many 'canonical' sound changes during this period. It offers an articulation between current trends in sociohistorical linguistics and wider debates in historiography. Where appropriate it brings to bear new syntheses such as that offered by Evolutionary Phonology. But, above all, the book aims to identify, examine, and explain the processes whereby speaker innovations develop into systemic changes in the language system. It can be seen in part as a response to a 'very exciting challenge' laid down by James Milroy over a decade ago: 'to link linguistic change with social change in such a way as to explain the conditions under which linguistic change takes on particular patterns...a very different task from that of orthodox historical linguistics' (Milroy 1992: 222).

1.1 Although linguists have frequently disagreed with each other over many phenomena in the history of English, there are some general points on which agreement is practically universal. First, present-day natural languages vary in ways which can in principle be described systematically, and presumably they did so in the past; human beings are still human beings. This axiom is known as the *uniformitarian hypothesis* (see Lass 1997: 25 and references cited there). To quote Suzanne Romaine, 'the linguistic forces which operate today and are observable around us are not unlike those which have operated in the past. Sociolinguistically speaking, this means that there is no reason for claiming that language did not vary in the same patterned ways in the past as it has been observed to do today' (Romaine 1982: 122–3; see also Machan 2003: 12). Such variation is to be expected in all levels of spoken language conventionally distinguished: lexicon, grammar, and phonology. Such variation is of course constrained: linguistic variants seem to arise in a set of ways which can be categorized, and this categorization of 'natural' variation has been a principal goal for linguists for many years (see Heggarty 2006: 187).

1.2 Secondly, all living languages have undergone change: 'languages which have no speakers do not change' (Milroy 1992: 4). Varieties of 'English' have been spoken continuously in some form or other since the Anglo-Saxons arrived in Britain in the fifth century AD, but Old English, with its distinctive inflectional system and handling of element order, is so different from Present-Day English that it has to be learned by modern students as practically a foreign language.

1.3 Less obviously, beginning students of Shakespeare can easily be deceived into thinking that Early Modern English is much the same as Present-Day English by the common editorial practice whereby seventeenth-century spellings and habits of punctuation are normalized according to present-day usage. However, such students rapidly realize that their understanding of the text is frequently obscured by distinctive lexical and grammatical usages which demonstrate that Shakespeare is hardly 'our contemporary' in linguistic terms. The same differences can be detected very clearly in pronunciation: scholarly research on speech from the early modern period shows, of course, that the accents in which Shakespeare is commonly delivered on the modern stage are very different from those in which his first audiences encountered him.

1.4 Languages vary, languages change: and a third point of common agreement amongst linguists is that there is connection between these two facts. But it is at this point that controversy occurs, for the articulation between variation and change is a complex matter, and scholars are not agreed as to how that articulation operates. It is an observable fact that some varieties of a given natural language are more 'conservative' than other varieties; thus speakers of Scots and Scottish English, for instance, still rhyme *good* and *food* as many of Shakespeare's contemporaries did (as is indicated by the spelling), whereas the two words no longer rhyme in southern British English. It is an observable fact that the sound [ŋ] is phonemic (and thus /ŋ/) in southern British English but a conditioned allophone of /n/ in accents from parts of the midlands and north of England. Thus the meaning of /sɪn/ and /sɪŋ/ is distinguished by the use of /n/ and /ŋ/ in the south, but [ŋ] is only found before /g/ in the north, e.g. [sɪŋg]: *sin* and *sing* are not, in many northern English accents, what is called a minimal pair. There is some evidence that *sin* and *sing* were not a minimal pair, either, for many Londoners in Shakespeare's day, and that /ŋ/ is therefore a new phoneme in the history of southern accents. Does this difference between apparently conservative and advanced accents mean that variation is not to be distinguished from change in progress, and that we can predict that northern accents will themselves adopt /ŋ/ as a distinct phoneme in a century or two, or that Scots in 2204 will no longer rhyme *good* and *food*?

1.5 There is also the question of evidence. Students of linguistic change are constantly frustrated by their inability to capture the precise moment of that change. We know that Shakespeare pronounced *meat* to rhyme with *mate*, whereas most speakers of British English now rhyme *meat* with *meet*: a sound change has occurred. However, whereas the moment when ice becomes water can be gauged precisely using a thermometer, the moment when *meat* changed its rhyme cannot be ascertained with similar precision.

1.6 Of course, such a desire is probably misplaced, for there are many natural phenomena which change so gradually that a precise moment of change is not to be had. A controversial example relates to childbirth: at what moment does the embryo become a human? Some would say at the moment of birth; others would say at the moment of conception. Legislators, in the unhappy position of having to make a decision, may decide on something like 22 or 24 weeks after conception, but before birth. Yet it seems at least arguable that the process whereby a human being diverges from its mother has to be seen not as a clear split but a process of becoming, where there is no precision about the time of separation. Indeed, it is at least arguable that the process of becoming a separate individual continues well beyond childbirth, as anyone with adolescent children, or who is an adolescent child, will know well.

1.7 Sound change, thankfully less morally complex, is, it is argued here, one of these gradual, processual, emergent phenomena. As with the emergence of a child, there is a small (indeed tiny) triggering moment, akin to the fertilisation of an egg with a sperm, but then a prolonged period akin to gestation and growth. It is also worth recalling that many fertilized eggs do not result in a live birth; similarly, many sound changes, it is suggested here, do not proceed very far. The purpose of this book is to explore—and, perhaps controversially, to explain—the processes involved in sound change in the history of early English in the light of this insight, showing how triggering and diffusion of change are linked.

1.8 If a processual model of sound change is accepted, there are certain implications for the historiographical method to be adopted. Formal models have many merits as synchronic, economical, snapshots, and can tell us many things about the inner workings of language. Thus, for instance, formalism can be used to demonstrate rather nicely the fact that certain kinds of change are regularly repeated in the history of individual languages (see e.g. Jones 1989). I shall be referring to recent important and enlightening formal approaches from time to time in this book, especially in Chapter 3. But such formal models are in principle not particularly new. Indeed, the classic 'laws' of Indo-European, such as the Laws of Grimm and Verner, are essentially formal descriptions, not explanations.

1.9 Most formal approaches seem not, and indeed are not intended, to take account of the historical contingency of sound change. As some of the examples already cited have indicated, the fact that sound change works at different speeds and in different ways in different areas suggests that some contingent, extralinguistic, historical, situation is involved in the process. Thus this book will be concerned with questions of contingency: why in that way? Why then? Why there?

1.10 In short, this book is an attempt to apply methods developed in modern historiography to historical linguistics. Such parasitism on other disciplines has been regularly practised by linguists, who have often adopted methods from philosophy or mathematics or the physical or biological or social sciences—or more notoriously their own conception of these disciplines—to account for the phenomena which interest them. However, as Roger Lass has put it, 'The most important point . . . is to know at all times exactly what we are doing' (Lass 1976: 220). The question therefore arises: what model of historiography is to be adopted? The last few years have seen a revolution among historians in the way in which they approach their craft, largely as a result of the impact of postmodernist thinking.

1.11 This book, it should be emphasized, is in no sense an attempt to transfer postmodernist thinking to historical linguistics; indeed, a postmodernist historical linguistics is rather hard to conceive of (though not impossible; the notion will be discussed explicitly, albeit very briefly, in the final chapter of this book). But mainstream historiography, though remaining sceptical about the postmodernist challenge, has been stimulated by postmodernism to rethink its theoretical underpinnings, most notably by Richard Evans (Evans 2000); and the processes involved in this rethinking have, it will be argued here, some relevance for historians who work with language. It is no coincidence that Evans has used a formulation of his goals very similar to that used by Lass: 'We all have to make some fundamental decisions about what we're doing nowadays before we do it. History is becoming a more theoretically and epistemologically self-conscious discipline, and that's all to the good.' (2000: 257)

1.12 Evans argues that 'making patterns and linkages, causal and otherwise, is by no means the only function of history, which also has a duty to establish the facts and recover the past in the present, but it is in the end what distinguishes it from chronicle' (Evans 2000: 252). The general argument of this book is that it is possible to make some tenable claims, always 'less than final' (Evans 2000: 253), about the origins and development of the early English sound changes which take on board not only general tendencies or 'drifts' in the language but also the specific contexts in which they are set.

1.13 I have chosen to look in particular at sound change in early English from a broadly 'philological' perspective because that is the subject and approach about which I have some, necessarily partial, knowledge; but it is hoped that readers of this book will be stimulated to debate the ideas presented here from their own perspectives. It is my belief that different approaches to a discipline are always, if variously, valid, and can only gain by entering into dialogue. It is in part for this reason that I have attempted to write this book with as little recourse to specialized formal and technical language as possible.

1.14 The remainder of this introductory chapter is concerned with exploring what is meant by the notion 'sound change', then examining three very influential studies in the field: Uriel Weinreich, William Labov and Marvin Herzog's ground-breaking article of 1968, 'Empirical foundations for a theory of language change'; the historical-sociolinguistic work of James Milroy, most thoroughly outlined in *Linguistic Variation and Change* (1992); and the multi-factorial approach developed by Michael Samuels in *Linguistic Evolution* (1972). I also identify certain pragmatic notions as being of crucial importance for the overall argument presented here, and then move on to discuss some important insights for understanding sound change which have arisen in recent work in phonetics.

2 What is sound change?

2.0 A simple-seeming answer to the question, 'What is sound change?', is as follows: a sound change is 'any appearance of a new phenomenon in the phonetic/phonological structure of a language' (Lass 1984: 315). But, like many simple answers, such a response provokes further questions. In this book, a sound change is assumed to take place when there has been a change in the system in which that sound exists and—a key point, it is argued here—where a change in sound involves a change in meaning, that is, when the 'deepest' level of language, namely, semantics, is in question. A starting-point, therefore, is to engage with this notion of systemic change.[1]

2.1 It is a truism, which has already been implicitly addressed above, that accents vary both in space and through time. It is thus necessary to develop a terminology to discuss this variation, allowing the organisation of accentual systems and comparison between different language states.

2.2 A starting-point for such a discussion is to be clear about the difference between phonology and phonetics. The science of phonetics is to do with the ways that sounds are made, that is, the whole process whereby air emitted from the lungs interacts with the various organs of the vocal tract. Phonology, on the other hand, is to do with the ways in which sounds are grouped to produce a meaningful utterance; thus we distinguish the meaning of *cat* and *pat* because the replacement of the sound represented by the letter *c* with one represented by the letter *p* changes the meaning of the word. The study of sound change has traditionally been focused on phonology, which is to do with systemic distinctions.

2.3 Phonological systems obviously vary between languages, and recent research has shown the huge range of possible systems

---

[1] Lass (1997: 281ff.) engages with the definition of change, but, interestingly, finds it hard to offer a clear definition. It is also interesting that Lass downplays issues of meaning in his 1997 study, and thus—as he very honestly admits—'largely evade[s]' questions of pragmatics, for instance' (1997: xviii). On semantics as the 'deepest' level of language, see, for instance, Smith (1996: ch. 1).

(see e.g. Ladefoged and Maddieson 1996: *passim*). But it is an observable fact that, even within languages, phonological systems vary. Thus, for instance, Scottish speakers of English have traditionally made a phonological distinction between the sounds represented by the spellings *w, wh* whereas Southern British English speakers, unless hypercorrecting on the basis of spelling, do not (cf. the pronunciation of the pair *witch, which* in these two varieties).

2.4 It is possible to classify such differences in ordered ways. It is traditional to distinguish *isolative* changes, where all sounds are affected whatever the environment, and *combinative* changes, which are environmentally conditioned, but this distinction is problematic if the point at issue is to do with systemic changes: if combinative changes are environmentally conditioned, are they real sound changes in the sense that they affect the linguistic system? Perhaps the clearest discussion of differences between accents has been set out by John Wells (1982: 72–80), who distinguishes *realizational, phonotactic, lexical–distributional,* and *systemic* differences. These differences can in turn be used as the basis for a categorization of sound change. Systemic and lexical–distributional changes are those phenomena which are most commonly considered when discussing sound changes. Thus a new phoneme may arise as the result of the phonemicization of original allophones (*splits*), or an old phonemic distinction may be lost (*mergers*); such changes are systemic changes. Redistributions of phonemes in the lexicon are known as *shifts*. An example of split is the emergence of a phonemic distinction between voiced and voiceless fricatives in the transition from Old to Middle English. Merger was evidently involved in the widespread loss of /x/ in the history of English (it now remains only in certain varieties of Scots, e.g. in *loch,* and even there is disappearing in the speech of younger people; see Lawson and Stuart-Smith 1999). Well-known lexical–distributional changes are Grimm's Law and the Great Vowel Shift. All these developments are discussed in subsequent chapters, where it will be observed that combinations are common, for example, 'split plus merger'.

2.5 However, realizational and phonotactic developments are also important, and need to be part of the study of the subject; and it is in this area that the boundary between phonetics and phonology becomes fuzzy. Loss of rhoticity, for instance, is a common phenomenon in the history of English (cf. present-day southern English with Scottish usage), while changes in the realization of /l/ have had (as will be argued in Chapter 4 below) important consequences for the history of contiguous sounds. These realizational and phonotactic developments have implications for better-known systemic (phonological) developments, and will be discussed at various points later in this book.

2.6 This categorization of changes will be accepted and referred to throughout this book. In the case studies which appear in later chapters, the notions split, merger and shift will be repeatedly referred to, and it will be observed that reference to one kind of change often connects with another. But it is worth asking precisely what kind of processes lie behind these metaphorical notions of 'split', 'merger', 'shift', and so on. Further, in some traditions of linguistic historiography such developments seem to happen without reference to the speakers who have effected these changes. What does a shift or a split or a merger mean in behavioural terms?

3 Speakers innovate, languages change

3.0 In order to address this behavioural question, it is necessary to clarify further what is meant by a language change: it is a matter of system, not of individual innovation, although individual innovation is a crucial prerequisite for change, and understanding language change, it is held here, requires an understanding of how it articulates with individual innovation.

3.1 Milroy has pointed out how important it is, in discussing the processes of change, to distinguish between speaker and system. He (1992: 5) tellingly cites Henry Wyld's dictum, 'The drama of linguistic change is enacted not in manuscripts or in inscriptions, but in the mouths and minds of men' (Wyld 1927: 21). Wyld's statement is interesting in a number of ways, but the reference to 'mouths and minds' is worth discussing at this point. Wyld seems to be distinguishing *utterance* ('mouths') and *mental framework* ('minds'); indeed, his distinction could be compared with the well-known distinction made by modern linguists between *performance* and *competence*.

3.2 Now, some linguists have not accepted that the study of performance or utterance or individual speakers is significant for the understanding of linguistic change. Roger Lass (1980: 120–2), for instance, expressing one traditional position, states that historical linguists generally look on language as 'an autonomous formal system', believing that it is 'languages that change and *not* speakers that change languages'. For Lass, the most productive approach to the subject is one which studies 'formal objects and their mutations over time, not . . . their inventors or users'. However, as Milroy observes, 'languages which have no speakers do not change; therefore it seems reasonable to inquire into the role of speakers in language change' (1992: 4).

3.3 Elsewhere (Smith 1996: 7–8), I have distinguished between *potential for change, implementation of change,* and *diffusion.* I have argued that potential for change lies in the linguistic variation, including innovations, continually produced by individual speakers; implementation takes place when one particular variant or set of variants is selected as part of a linguistic system of a particular speech community; and diffusion takes place when that system is adopted by speech communities beyond the original group. Thus the potential for change is always present, in the set of variants within a given linguistic system. However, a particular interaction of processes—*extralinguistic* with *intralinguistic,* with subsequent further intralinguistic interactions—at a particular time and in a particular place triggers the implementation of change, with subsequent diffusion of that change beyond its original point of actuation.

3.4 Although my categorization, it is held here, remains broadly valid, it must be admitted that it can be misinterpreted as suggesting discreteness rather than continuity between each stage—a common problem in categorization, as is witnessed, for example, by the notorious difficulties that cultures have in distinguishing boundaries between different colours. To put the problem another way, such a categorization is rather like using a series of still photographs to record three stages in the movement of a given object: such stills, rather like a Muybridge record of a running man or a galloping horse, give us useful information but cannot capture the true nature of movement.

3.5 Moreover, the categorization deals entirely with language-internal phenomena: variants, innovations, language-internal systems. Yet the evidence is that such phenomena cannot be properly separated from discussion of the users of this linguistic material: speakers and the dynamic, complex, speech-communities of which they are part. Speakers innovate, but they also hear other speakers innovating and may attempt, for various reasons, to imitate them; and, if they attempt to imitate the innovation of another speaker through this monitoring process, can this adoption be said to be a linguistic change?

3.6 The answer offered here is that it is precisely this moment of adoption which marks a linguistic change, for adoption presupposes at least partial understanding, and understanding in turn presupposes a grasp of the linguistic system through which meaning of various kinds can be communicated; there is an iterative relationship between speaker and system. (Thus, it might be argued, an approach which is wholly usage-based or system-based misses a key component: both aspects of language need to be addressed.) Such meaning of course includes not just information-sharing but also such phenomena as assertion of social position or group solidarity. Therefore a definition of a speech community would require at least two speaker–hearers, and a linguistic change can be said to have occurred when an innovation is adopted—consciously or (more commonly) unconsciously—by a second speaker-hearer and—this is a crucial point—has a systemic effect. In other words, a linguistic change occurs when a second speaker adopts, or attempts to adopt, a *systemic* feature of another speaker and their system, in turn, changes—a point which will be developed further later in this chapter.

3.7 The notion that a speech community can consist of as few as two people, and that the implementation of a linguistic change occurs when an innovation is adopted by one person other than the innovator, may strike some readers as rather absurd or extreme. But it is important to recall at this point the third stage in the categorization: diffusion. It may well be that many, if not most, linguistic changes as just defined are never diffused very far.

3.8 We have all encountered 'family usages'—often special meanings of words or phrases—which are shared within small social units but never go much beyond them. Most married couples have private usages peculiar to themselves, not shared beyond the couple concerned, which nevertheless have a systemic, meaningful character.

3.9 Such usages are stable to the group concerned, of course. However, it is noticeable that when outsiders first join the group misunderstanding can easily follow. An anecdote from my own experience might help clarify the point. When I first met my wife's family I noted the expression 'I'm not fussed about that'—a usage which was not really part of my repertoire—and assumed, based on my previously acquired knowledge of English idiom, that it implied indifference to a particular course of action or pattern of behaviour. It was some time before I grasped that it meant *hostility* to that action or behaviour. As an outsider, my links to the group were initially weaker, and I was therefore more likely to misunderstand the meaning of utterances special to the close-knit group I was joining.

3.10 I have now adopted the expression within the family group; my usage has therefore changed. Of course, if I had not sustained the link through marriage it would have been possible for me to adopt the expression as part of my own linguistic repertoire while remaining ignorant of its precise meaning *for the group from which I had derived it*. Such a mistaken adoption would have represented a linguistic innovation, and—as will be discussed in later chapters—such mistakes, or perhaps better, 'near-misses', have been identified as the primary mechanism involved in linguistic change (see Section 6).

3.11 Such linguistic changes, of course, remain private, not open to observation by historical (or indeed other) linguists, and it is only if we accept—as few do—a teleological view of linguistic history that we might find implausible the notion of an innovating system failing to 'catch on'. Indeed, there is some evidence that even changes which enter the historical record can have a limited life-span, such as the rise and fall of the *do*-periphrasis during the Early Modern English period, or the Early Middle English emergence of a competing case-based determiner system (see Smith 1996: ch. 7 and references there), or the temporary accession of vocabulary items, as attested very frequently in the *Oxford English Dictionary*.

3.12 It therefore seems theoretically robust to suggest that many linguistic changes fail to diffuse beyond a very limited speech community, and that only the most egregious examples are accessible to scholarly attention. Such a profile for change fits rather well, too, with the widely accepted model for diffusion of change, the 'S-curve', whereby change begins to spread slowly at first with rapid pick-up only later in the cycle (see Figure 1.1). Obviously, this book will be concerned mainly with examples further along the S-curve, but the very beginnings of a change would certainly make an interesting programme for further diachronic research. In most cases these beginnings would irretrievable, of course, though some recent work in the field would repay closer attention from this perspective (see e.g. Trudgill 1999).

3.13 Thus a sound change may be defined as follows:

Sound change
A sound change has taken place when a variant form, mechanically produced, is imitated by a second person and that process of imitation causes the system of the imitating individual to change.

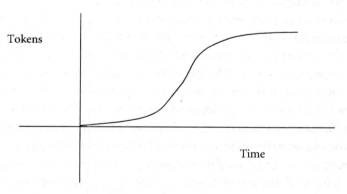

FIGURE 1.1 S-curve model for diffusion of change

We will return to this formulation, and its implications, regularly in this book.

4 Insights from pragmatics and sociolinguistics

4.0 This extremely limited conception of the speech-community—more than one person—articulates with the insights which students of pragmatics have brought to linguistic enquiry. Pragmatics, which may be defined as 'the study of how utterances have meanings in situations' (Leech 1983: x), can be taken as a complementary discipline to sociolinguistics: both disciplines are concerned, from different perspectives, with language use.

4.1 A crucial insight of pragmatics has been the notion of accommodation, which relates any given linguistic act to the relationship between particular interlocutors, derived from H. P. Grice's Cooperative Principle. Grice's Principle holds that, to communicate with someone else it is necessary to cooperate with that person linguistically; and, to cooperate with that person linguistically, it is necessary to use language in the same way as that person is using it. It is often said that long-married husbands and wives end up looking like each other because they spend so much time unconsciously mimicking each other's facial expressions; something similar seems to happen with linguistic behaviour.

4.2 To account for further diffusion, and incidentally to make a link with sociolinguistics, another pragmatic notion is useful: accommodation theory. Accommodation theory holds that any particular usage at any particular point in time is the result of an 'act of identity', in which speakers are seen as modifying their behaviour to accommodate to group norms. Thus, 'the individual creates for himself the patterns of his linguistic behaviour so as to resemble those of the group or groups with which from time to time he wishes to be identified, or so as to be unlike those from whom he wishes to be distinguished' (Le Page and Tabouret-Keller 1985: 181).

4.3 The notion of accommodation acts as a link between pragmatics and sociolinguistics. It may be related to a notion commonly employed by sociologists and, by extension, sociolinguists: the notion of 'ties' within social networks, which Milroy (1992: *passim*) considers of central importance for understanding language change. Individuals are all to a greater or lesser extent linked to the communities of which they are part, and communities can be categorized by the nature of those ties. Strongly tied communities are typically long-established, manifesting little social change but a great deal of close social contact; weakly tied communities are typically comparatively recently established, manifesting much social change and broad rather than deep social contacts.

4.4 It is fairly clear that the pool of linguistic variants—the size of 'variational spaces'—available in weakly tied communities will be larger than in strongly tied communities; it is also likely that innovatory usages will be more widespread in the former rather than in the latter. We might therefore expect change to be more rapid and more extreme in weakly tied communities and indeed, as James Milroy showed from his work, with Lesley Milroy, on Belfast speech (1992: ch. 6), this pattern is borne out by observation. Very broadly put, innovation seems to be faster or more extreme in rapidly growing towns and cities and in areas where settlement has been recent; innovation seems to be slower in rural areas and in traditional urban communities where communities need strong social ties for mutual support.

4.5 These notions also allow us to define more precisely what is meant by the notion of 'speech community'. Boundaries between speech communities are not (except with communities completely isolated for geographical reasons from the outside world, as in parts of South America or South-East Asia) clear-cut. Individuals within speech communities have systems of language, but these systems will allow for variation in speech in different circumstances, and it is quite possible for individuals to operate a number of systems. The notion 'speech community' is a valuable one, but it is important to be aware that it represents a focus of usages within a continuum of utterance. In short, speech communities are dynamic, shifting phenomena (see Kretzschmar 2002).

5 The actuation problem

5.0 This book is of course hardly the first to address the question of historical contingency in language change. Perhaps the most influential study of the subject has been Weinreich, Labov, and Herzog (1968), which puts the question starkly: 'Why do changes in a structural feature take place in a particular language at a given time, but not in other languages with the same feature, or in the same language at other times?' (1968: 102) This question formulates what is known as *the actuation problem*, which Weinreich *et al.* regarded as 'the heart of the matter'.

5.1 The actuation problem has been a major challenge to historical linguists, and has produced various responses. Some scholars have regarded the problem as simply insoluble or uninteresting, and have therefore set it aside; this response is often associated with those who have approached the study of past language states wholly from what is known as a 'language-internal' viewpoint. And indeed, the formulation offered by Weinreich *et al.* is a challenging one. James Milroy has pointed out that 'The actuation problem... is so challenging that historical linguists do not usually address it directly; this is hardly surprising as, when it is formulated in this way, it is actually insoluble: a solution to it implies the capacity to *predict*, not only what particular change will happen, but also when and where it will happen. However the probability of any event in life actually taking place at some particular and specified place and time is close to zero.' (1992: 20)[2]

---

[2] It is important to make a distinction between actuation and later stages in the diffusion of a sound change, even if the dividing-line is hard to distinguish in practice. Actuation is to do with triggering of a change; implementation is to do with the process whereby the change works its way through a given system. Indeed, 'inception' is often seen as to do with the process whereby a change, once triggered, is implemented. Thus, for instance, important discussions of (say) the Great Vowel Shift often proceed by describing the process of raising of (say) mid-vowels. I would regard this process of raising as the implementation of the change, whereas actuation is to do with the triggering of the raising.

5.2 Milroy, however, goes on to draw an analogy with meteor-ology:

Weather prediction is a convenient analogy here: we can predict from meteorological observations that it will rain on a particular day with a high probability of being correct, but if we predict that in a particular place it will start raining at one minute past eleven and stop at six minutes past twelve, the probability of the prediction being correct is vanishingly low. Nevertheless, we would be bad meteorologists if we did not try to improve the accuracy of our predictions, and of course this greater accuracy includes the ability to specify the conditions under which something will not happen as well as the conditions under which it will happen. In view of all this, we have no excuse as linguists for not addressing the actuation problem.   (1992: 20–1)

5.3 And it is possible, of course, that the emphasis on prediction as a goal for historical linguists has been overstated, and here insights from general historiography are helpful. Historians, or perhaps more properly users of history, are notoriously poor predictors of future events: 'nothing in human society...ever happens twice under exactly the same conditions or in exactly the same way... historians are no more capable of imagining or predicting the future accurately than anyone else' (Evans 2000: 59, 229). It seems best, therefore, to take a very general view of the requirement for predictability, along lines such as follows:

Predictability

There are several factors and processes that can be involved in a particular language change at a particular time, and these factors and processes are such and such; however, the interaction between these factors and processes is so complex and so various that exact predictability is not to be had. The precise nature of the interaction of these factors and processes can, it seems, only be distinguished after the event.

5.4 The factors and processes involved, it is held here, are to do with pragmatic interaction between individuals, who are to a greater or lesser extent socially 'tied'. Since it seems likely, from Milroy's research, that change happens more rapidly and more profoundly during the moment of interaction between weakly tied individuals it is possible to offer a scenario much as follows:

Language Change

A given language change results from the interaction between two individuals. One attempts, consciously or (more probably) unconsciously, to imitate the usage of the other, for reasons of peer-identification. If the individuals become strongly tied socially (e.g. within a family group, or in a close-knit work group) the usage is imitated precisely. However if the individuals are weakly tied socially, one speaker may 'miss the target' because weak ties do not allow for persistent monitoring of linguistic behaviour. The 'mistaken' outcome can then be passed to another individual. Of course, it is possible that several individuals behave in the same or in similar ways for the same reason, viz., group identification; if such group behaviour occurs, then we might expect the change to be diffused more vigorously or sustained.

6 Hyperadaptation and hypoadaptation

6.0 The notion of the 'missed target' has been well-established in the scholarly literature, and was identified by Michael Samuels over thirty years ago (e.g. 1972: 10). More recently, as the result of detailed work by John Ohala (e.g. 1993) and Bjorn Lindblom (e.g. 1990), it has become known as the 'H&H' theory. 'H&H' refers to *hypo-* and *hyperarticulation*, which might, in terms of this book, be rephrased as *hypo-* and *hyperadaptation*. Listeners, when reproducing the sounds they hear, under- (*hypo-*) or overshoot (*hyper-*) their target; in other words, they replicate imperfectly what they hear. Lindblom (1986: 499) sums up the process as follows: 'speakers have the freedom to vary, that is to elaborate (overarticulate) or simplify (underarticulate) their speech under the control of communicative and situational constraints.'

6.1 Hypo-/hyperadaptation has sometimes been considered to be a marginal phenomenon. However, it is held here to be a key process in linguistic change, and it will be observed as such in the discussions of examples which form the core of this book.

6.2 The terms *hypo-/hyperadaptation* should not be confused with the better-known term *hypercorrection*. Kinds of hypo-/hyperadaptation include hypercorrection, an inaccurate attempt to reproduce a form regarded as prestigious within a speech community. Such prestige can (to use the traditional term) be *overt*, that is, assigned to a usage which is widely adopted or approved of in educational or media-led practice, for instance British 'Received Pronunciation'. Usages can also be *covertly* prestigious, that is, associated with social groups whose prestige in society does not derive from educationally enforced norms. However, hypo-/hyperadaptation also includes *hyperdialectalism*, where a speaker attempts inaccurately to reproduce a form characteristic of the locale to which he or she has moved, in an attempt to identify with speakers there. It is for this reason that accommodation theory is important; hypo-/hyperadaptors *wish to be like their interlocutors*.

6.3 How the H&H process works in sound change is fairly well-established in the literature, and indeed it derives from much earlier formulations; as G. L. Brook put it in a classic student handbook from the 1940s, 'There remain...many sound-changes for which one can discover no further cause than successive inaccurate imitations on the part of several generations of speakers of a language' (Brook 1947: 5). Here the insights of modern phoneticians are crucial, from both articulatory and acoustic perspectives (see Samuels 1972: ch. 2 and *passim*, and, with considerable thoroughness and sophistication, Stuart-Smith 2004: *passim*).

6.4 We might recall Lindblom's words (see 6.0 above): 'speakers have the freedom to vary, that is to elaborate (overarticulate) or simplify (underarticulate) their speech under the control of communicative and situational constraints'. In other words, speakers have a repertoire of variant realizations for a given item from which they can select. Particular situations (e.g. emphatic speech, relaxed speech) will cause speakers to adopt particular realizations from the repertoire available to them (see Samuels 1972: 21ff.). However, within these repertoires, speakers will have prototypical norms of pronunciation around which the realizations of particular phonemes cluster. Indeed, one older definition of the notion *phoneme* relates to this clustering around norms—'a family of related sounds' in the words of Daniel Jones (1956: 172)—rather than to the set of oppositions derived from minimal pairs. (For a schematic illustration of the notion *families of sounds*, see Figure 1.2.)

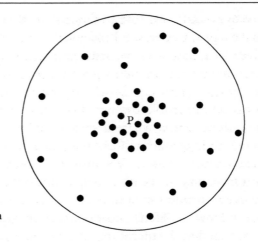

● = actual realizations

P = prototypical realization

FIGURE 1.2 Families of sounds

6.5 The precise prototypical articulation of sounds varies from speaker to speaker; speakers understand each other because there is, in the listening process, a broad tolerance of a good deal of variation. This process of interaction between articulatory and acoustic processes has been discussed by Dennis Fry, and an extended quotation from Fry's work makes the point very effectively (1979: 129):

> ...the sounds of speech are extremely variable, that is to say that when a number of different speakers utter the 'same' word, the sounds are acoustically different in many respects. In spite of this it is very rarely that we have any difficulty in recognizing a word spoken to us; as listeners we are very well practised in arriving at the right answer when taking in a message in the face of a wide range of variation in the acoustic signals. Two factors are mainly responsible for our ability to do this: first, whenever someone is talking to us, we have a very good idea of what to expect; from our knowledge of the language, of the person talking and of the general situation we are able to predict more or less the course the message will follow. This property of speech and of language which makes such prediction possible is referred to technically as *redundancy*...the second factor which accounts for our success in dealing with the variability of speech is our capacity for discarding quite a proportion of this information and pinning our attention to a few selected acoustic features. These features...are called *acoustic cues*.

6.6 Fry goes on to point out that 'there is substantial evidence that English listeners, for instance, do not all use the same cues for a given distinction' (1979: 130), and this perception has been developed in recent work in the field of accent studies. D. B. Pisoni (1997: 10) notes, for instance, that 'the human perception and memory systems appear to encode and retain very fine details of the perceptual event.' In such circumstances, all sorts of distinctions can be made and perceived. Paul Foulkes and Gerard Docherty, in the introduction to an important set of essays on this subject (Foulkes and Docherty 1999), note that such variation 'plays a key role in our everyday perception of ourselves and our interlocutors. It may affect our success in communication, and our job prospects' (1999: 23).

6.7 Hypo-/hyperadaptation classically occurs when two speakers with distinct systems encounter each other, and one attempts, for some reason, to change his or her accent in order to identify with the other's prototypical norms. Thus, in British English, speakers who habitually 'drop their aitches' may insert /h/ before word-initial vowels even when such an /h/ is not required in RP, for instance *hi* for *I*. In Wells's terminology, this development could be regarded as a lexical–distributional change or shift; other changes (splits, mergers) can similarly be triggered by hypo-/hyperadaptive behaviour. It is argued in this book that such adaptations, deriving from contact between speakers, are important triggers for linguistic change. It seems likely, too, that the process is further encouraged by the frequency with which such triggering takes place: 'there is growing evidence that token frequency plays an important role in the acquisition of sound patterns' (Blevins 2004: 37, and references cited there; see especially the essays collected in Bybee and Hopper 2001).

7 Contact

7.0 The notion of *contact* has been raised; but it needs some unpacking at this point, since it has traditionally been taken by linguistic historians to refer to large-scale contact between distinct communities, such as Received Pronunciation and non-Received Pronunciation speakers, or Norsemen and Anglo-Saxons.

7.1 It is an observable fact that communities with little contact with the outside world undergo language change very slowly. Perhaps the best-known example of this phenomenon, discussed by James and Lesley Milroy (1985), is Icelandic, which has changed remarkably little since the Middle Ages, apparently as a consequence of the close-knit social structure of the inhabitants combined with the country's comparative isolation as an island in the middle of the North Atlantic. Whereas Early Middle English, the contemporary of recorded Old Icelandic, is very different from Present-Day English, present-day Icelanders have little difficulty in making sense of the substantial Icelandic prose saga-literature which survives from the thirteenth century. The difference seems to derive from the fact that Icelandic has adopted comparatively little usage (pronunciation, grammar, vocabulary) from other languages, whereas English has borrowed a great deal from Norse, French, etc.

7.2 Rather less appreciated is that contact between varieties of the 'same' language can cause change. The most obvious examples are to do with processes of standardization, whereby a set of usages is adopted (or misadopted) by a community because that set of usages is perceived to be socially prestigious. Such changes, both between languages and between varieties of the same language, are referred to as *exogenous changes*.

7.3 Observations such as these just made suggest that linguistic change is contact-induced, and indeed this argument underpins the work of, for instance, James Milroy. However, Peter Trudgill, in his study of present-day usage in Norwich, England, has drawn attention to a number of changes which he regards as *endogenous*, that is, 'which appear to be internal to the system itself' (1999: 134). Perhaps the best-known of these changes is the fronting of /uː/ in GOAT, a realizational change whereby the vowel [ʊu] is replaced by [ʉu]. Such changes, Trudgill states, 'are without parallel anywhere in neighbouring or metropolitan or national prestige varieties...We seem forced to accept the possibility that change can be truly system-internal' (1999: 139).

7.4 The GOAT change is remarkable since it can be dated very precisely. Trudgill did not notice it in his original fieldwork in Norwich, which he carried out in 1968. It was first distinguished by William Labov in 1971, when he analysed the speech of two boys, 'friends aged 11' (Trudgill 1999: 135), who had been too young to take part in Trudgill's original survey. Trudgill notes that '[this] pronunciation, which has now become the norm amongst younger Norwich speakers, did not occur at all in my 1968 example, in which the youngest speakers were born in 1958. We are therefore able to say with an unusual degree of accuracy that it first occurred in Norwich English in the speech of those born around 1960' (1999: 135). Trudgill has suggested that such findings—he draws attention to other similar developments, such as the diphthongization of the vowel in words such as TRAP, and the merger of the NEAR and SQUARE vowels—would 'shed some doubt on the argument (see Milroy 1992) that all change is the result of contact' (1999: 134).

7.5 However, it is possible that the notion of *system* adopted by Trudgill is too narrowly based, and that the notion of endogenous change (as opposed to exogenous/externally influenced change) needs qualification. It may be recalled that change has been defined above as happening when one speaker adopts the innovation of another; all societies, however homogenous, have dynamics within them which mean that power relations can change in a very delicate way on a micro-level. It might be noted in passing that the development Trudgill cited was first observed in the speech of two 11-year-old friends; the pragmatic relations to do with that friendship, and the group of peers within which that friendship existed, are (understandably) not retrievable from Trudgill's account. However, William Labov's own work on the power structures, and their linguistic correlates, obtaining in Harlem (New York) gangs suggests some models for such groups within which the imitation of an innovation of the kind Trudgill describes might be adopted (see Labov 1972: passim); similar effects have been noted in many communities (e.g. Eleanor Lawson's and Jane Stuart-Smith's study of variation between /x/ and /k/ in Glaswegian schools; see Lawson and Stuart-Smith 1999; Stuart-Smith 1999). It is not a coincidence that many of these studies are to do with the speech of children and adolescents, whose social relationships are notoriously open to flux.

7.6 What Trudgill's findings suggest is that we must always accept, in our theorizing, that a change can emerge without large-scale contact between distinct communities with distinct phonological systems. However, such a conclusion does not, it is argued here, negate the centrality of contact as a mechanism of linguistic change. If a linguistic change can be said to take place when one speaker imitates another, consciously or unconsciously, then any innovation adopted by another as a result of peer-identification can be said to be the result of contact. Changes which are not widely imitated and diffused may remain unobserved—'under the radar'—and may ultimately fizzle out; changes which are widely imitated and diffused will proceed further along the S-curve and will become available for scholarly analysis. The issue, it is argued here, is simply one of scale, not of the mechanism involved.

7.7 One further, very important, point should be made which derives from this discussion: we must presume that the triggering of sound change, ultimately, is not accessible to precise scholarly identification. We know where to look, but identifying the precise moment of contact can be like looking for a needle in a haystack. April McMahon (1994: 251–2) describes this as a situation where 'we now know where to look, but can't see anything'. But, it is argued here, this should not preclude us from seeking causes of change.

8 Systemic regulation

8.0 In the light of the argument so far, the question naturally arises as to why some changes are widely imitated while others are not. The answer lies in the systematic character of language, though the notion of *system* needs some unpacking; as we saw from Trudgill's example, it can be rather narrowly envisaged. *System* should, it is argued here, be used in a broad sense, referring not only to 'language-internal' relations (vocabulary, grammar, sound system) but also to the location of language in relation to social context (see Firth 1957: 8–11 for some interesting insights on this issue, and also Lass 1997: 352–3 for a critique of a limited view of systems). Thus questions of systemic change relate not only to (say) the impact of sound change on grammar, but also to such processes as standardization and levelling. If language is not conceived of in this way then it is hard to understand how it can be used for communicative purposes.

8.1 As I have discussed elsewhere (Smith 1996: 5 and *passim*), languages are systems in which everything is connected to everything else (*tout se tient*, in the words of Saussure, Grammont, and their followers; see Koerner 1999: ch. 10). This structural notion has been the major insight of linguistics since the modern discipline was founded in the nineteenth century, and underpins its scientific status. If this notion is accepted, disturbance must therefore have consequences for the rest of the system as broadly conceived. To return to the simple example from my own experience: since 'I'm not fussed about that' now expresses hostility to a given suggestion or notion in my family circle, I cannot again use the expression, within the family circle, if my intention is to flag indifference. Such restructuring processes result in a changed system; a process of systemic regulation has been undertaken.

8.2 A proper understanding of the process of systemic regulation requires a grasp of the complex relationship between linguistic form and linguistic function. As will be seen repeatedly in the discussions which follow, and will be returned to in more detail in the final chapter, function constrains form. Which forms or sets of forms from the pool available are selected for use at a given point in time seems to be determined by the function within the system which is required. The overall direction of change results from the complex and dynamic interaction of extra- and intralinguistic developments: a 'hidden hand' or 'blind watchmaker' effect (Keller 1994; see further Smith 1996: ch. 9). To put matters another way, forms arise by *chance* (although constrained by certain general phonetic tendencies), and are the outcome of historical contingency. However, which forms survive is a matter of *choice* (see further Blevins 2004, and Chapter 3).

8.3 Such notions, moreover, can be linked quite effectively with recent 'emergentist' theories of change. Emergence is a notion which plays an important role in all physical and biological sciences. MacWhinney (2001: 450), for instance, draws attention to the formation of the patterned hexagons which make up a honeycomb:

When a bee returns to the hive after collecting pollen, she deposits a drop of wax-coated honey. Initially, each of these honey balls is round and of approximately the same size. As these balls get packed together, they take on the familiar hexagonal shape that we see in the honeycomb. There is no gene in the bee that codes for hexagonality in the honeycomb, nor is there any overt communication regarding the shaping of the cells of the honeycomb. Rather, this form is an emergent consequence of the application of packing rules to a collection of honey balls of roughly the same size...

In other words, the hexagons have arisen through systemic regulation. Wax-coated honey-balls have no intrinsic intelligence; no 'intelligent designer' is needed to explain the resulting hexagonal pattern. Similarly, no intelligent designer is needed to explain the emergence of new linguistic structures; structures arise of their own accord. As Roger Lass puts it, 'blind, non-teleological, dumb and boring processes can lead to order, design and even purpose' (1997: 380).

8.4 But it is important to emphasize that the forms which contribute to this pattern are the outcome of historical contingency. The long neck of the giraffe fulfils a role, enabling (it seems) male giraffes to use their heads as weapons, rather like golf clubs or polo sticks, in the competition for mates or grazing, but the long neck did not arise for that specific purpose. It arose through mutation; it then developed a function, and was favoured. To repeat: forms arise by historical contingency; which forms survive relates to choice constrained—but not directed—by function. In other words, a variant arises mechanically, but is then favoured (or not) within the system of which it is a part. (See, for a developed evolutionary parallel, McMahon 2000a, especially Chapter 4; for a useful survey of the issues involved, see McMahon 1994: ch. 12.)

8.5 Of course, this functional explanation cannot be pushed too far. In nature there are many features which had a function once but no longer do so, such as the human appendix, or the male human nipple, which has an embryological function but remains after the embryo develops sexual difference. These residualisms survive, it could be argued, simply through evolutionary inertia; they have no special function but nor are they generally dysfunctional, even if they can on occasion cause problems, as with burst appendices (for an extended discussion of the relevance of the male nipple, see Lass 1997: 12–13). It seems likely that, in linguistic evolution, there are similarly 'functionally neutral' phenomena. Therapeutic change only operates, it seems, when it is necessary.[3]

8.6 This insight enables us, it may be argued, to develop a robust definition of sound change, which was defined in 3.13 as follows: *a sound change has taken place when a variant form, mechanically produced, is imitated by a second person and that process of imitation causes the system of the imitating individual to change.*

8.7 Thus a study of sound change requires both phonetic and phonological concerns to be brought together.

9 The structure of this book

9.0 Taken together, the three mechanisms of variation, contact, and systemic regulation form a general theoretical framework for the study of sound change and are seen as essential for the understanding of the phenomenon.

9.1 The remainder of this book falls into three parts. Chapter 2 discusses the problems of evidence which confront the student

---

[3] For an important discussion of the status of the functional approach, see the essays in Koopman *et al.* (1987), especially those by Jean Aitchison, Roger Lass, and M. L. Samuels; see also McMahon (1994: *passim*). Lass returns to the debate in Lass (1997: ch. 7, *passim*). The debate is a fascinating one, not least because it forces readers to engage with very basic questions of explanation and teleology in linguistic change. I have attempted to address the question generally in Smith (1996), though Lass's (1997) discussion provides some important new challenges.

My own view is that Lass downplays the semiotic function of language. Thus his well-known example of 'anti-functionalist' *shit* 'shut' < Old English *scyttan*, clashing with *shit* 'excrement', becomes clear once it is realized that the word has actually changed its connotations over time, and that the *shit* 'shut' form seems to drop out of use at broadly the same time that the *shit* 'excrement' form becomes stigmatized. See Lass (1997: 355), but also Smith (1996: 138–9) for an example of 'non-taboo' *shit* in Middle English. Theoretically relevant arguments are presented in Anttila (1989).

of sound change in the history of English. Chapter 3 deals with phonological processes and models. It exemplifies splits, mergers and shifts from the history of English and (indeed) pre-English, and then goes on to discuss some of the models which English historical linguists have used to map these processes. It concludes with an extended discussion of one major development in the pre-English period, Grimm's Law.

9.2 These opening chapters are followed by three chapters (Chapters 4 through 6), each specifically focussed on one well-known sound change in the history of English, namely, Breaking (ch. 4), processes of lengthening (ch. 5), and what may be termed the Great Vowel Shifts (ch. 6). These chapters are ordered on roughly chronological grounds; thus Chapter 4 deals with the period when English emerged as a language distinct from the other West Germanic varieties, Chapter 5 is to do with processes which are particularly salient in the transition from Old to Middle English, and Chapter 6 is concerned with a defining difference between Middle and Early Modern English. This ordering of material, fairly obviously, is intended to show how our explanations become more plausible as evidence for the processes involved becomes more plentiful.

9.3 It will be observed that Chapters 2 through 6 deal with many of the major sound changes during the early English period, very broadly defined as from the origins of the language to *c.*1700. However, this book is not intended as a conventional history of English phonology, for which see standard textbooks, such as the *Cambridge History of the English Language*/Hogg *et al.* 1992–2001/or single-volume surveys such as Prins (1974) and Jones (1989). Also recommended is Wells (1982), which includes a valuable historically oriented section on 'residualisms'. To help less advanced readers, an Appendix of sound changes is supplied at the end of this book (Appendix 1). The last chapter of the book returns to the general arguments of this introduction, and makes some suggestions about possible ways forward for the study of the subject.

2

On Evidence

1 Witnesses

1.0 The previous chapter offered a model for understanding sound change, based on observations derived from Present-Day English. However, there are some major problems with transferring present-day approaches to linguistic variation and change to past states of the language. The most obvious of these is to do with evidence; in this chapter, an attempt is made to show how historical development in relation to language can be researched, given the limitations of the evidence available.

1.1 All history begins with the study of evidence: the analysis of primary sources, including a critical assessment of their value. For historians, such primary sources are of two kinds: artefacts (e.g. buildings, weapons, other surviving physical objects), and comments by contemporaries surviving in contemporary or near-contemporary documents. Questions of evidence are also involved in the historical study of language: the study of artefacts in context (e.g. manuscripts and inscriptions, or—from the late nineteenth century—recorded speech), or the examination of contemporary comments on linguistic behaviour (e.g. the writings of the sixteenth-century orthoepists). Texts do not come down to us without contexts, and, as Robert D. Fulk has pointed out, 'the study of historical linguistics may be founded on delusive presuppositions when it is conducted outside of any actual historical contextualization of the texts in which the data are preserved' (Fulk 1996: 508). Such materials require, in short, forensic examination.

1.2 The courtroom analogy, whereby scholars use the term *witnesses* to refer to primary sources, is a useful one, not least because it reminds us of the limitations of evidence (see Lass 1997: 19). As all lawyers—and indeed all historians—know, witnesses can be partial or even misleading without careful probing, and the same goes for our informants for early pronunciation. Moreover, historical linguists have no mechanism of quality control for their informants; they have to make do with the various pieces of evidence which have survived the vagaries of time, and of course their informants cannot be interrogated orally as in a courtroom. And scholars of more recent history in particular can suffer from information overload, the problem by which interpretation of events is made complex by the sheer mass of material available.

1.3 Before the arrival of sound-recording, four sources of witnesses are traditionally distinguished for past states of the sound system of a language: writing systems, verse practices, contemporary writers on language, and information arrived at through the process known as reconstruction. In this chapter, issues relating to all four will be discussed.

2 Writing systems

2.0 English has been transmitted for the last 1500 years in two ways: by speech, which is evanescent, and through writing, which is comparatively permanent. Speech and writing are both methods of transmission, and in that sense they map onto the 'same' grammatical and lexical structures, but the distinction between evanescence and permanence means that the two modes of transmission are likely to diverge in important ways. The mapping of sound onto symbol is not after all a natural one: for instance, <w> maps onto [w] for an English speaker, but onto [v] for a German. There is, in short, nothing intrinsically sound-symbolic about a letter; communities have simply agreed, as they do when assigning values to money (coins, paper), to assign sound values to particular symbols.

2.1 This point was noted by the grammarians of antiquity such as Donatus and Priscian, who developed the 'doctrine of *littera*'. According to this doctrine, distinctions were made between *figura* (symbol), *potestas* (sound equivalent) and *nomen* (name of the letter), with *littera* (letter) as the overall superordinate. More recently, linguists have developed a four-fold system of definition which allows for distinctions between underlying form and contextual realization: phonemes and allophones, graphemes and allographs.

2.2 Just as we distinguish between phonemes and allophones in sound-systems, so we distinguish between graphemes and allographs in writing systems. A grapheme may be defined as the abstract form, e.g. <a>; an allograph is the realization of that form in a particular environment (e.g. font, script or position in a word). Thus ≪a, a, a, a, a and a≫ are all allographs. Similarly, in many Middle English scripts, ≪v≫ and ≪u≫ are allographs of <v>, ≪v≫ being used in initial position and ≪u≫ being used in medial position.

2.3 A further distinction is generally made between logographic and phonographic writing systems. Phonographic writing systems, where sounds map onto sound-segments or onto syllables, are an attempt to capture the original evanescence of one aspect of human experience, language, in comparatively permanent form. The separate operation of writing is much more clearly marked in logographic systems (such as that adopted in Chinese), where written symbols map not onto sounds but onto the meanings sounds and written symbols both attempt to transmit.

2.4 Writing systems, indeed, are designed to be 'fit for purpose', and those purposes can change. Logographic systems, such as that used for Chinese, operate rather like money: they form a shared currency for the socio-political purpose of unifying peoples with very different spoken forms. Thus a Cantonese speaker will not be able to understand the speech of a speaker of Mandarin, but each will be able to read the other's writings; the disadvantage for both is that many symbols are needed, but these disadvantages are seen as trade-offs in social terms.[4]

2.5 Phonographic systems are much more economical, in that a limited set of symbols is needed; thus English speakers and French speakers use what is (essentially) the same alphabet. However, without learning the other language, it is not possible for English readers to understand French writing, and vice versa. In sum, there is a trade-off between economy and communicative power, with the users of written languages making different choices depending on social functions. There is therefore nothing particularly 'natural' about alphabetic systems, such as that used for Present-Day English, where symbols map broadly onto sound-segments; indeed, it has been pointed out that all such systems seem to go back to a single moment of human invention, whereas logographic systems seem to have been invented separately in a number of places, as do phonographic systems where symbols map onto syllables (see further Ladefoged 2001: 171–3).

2.6. In an ideal phonographic system, phonemes map onto graphemes; allophonic representation in a writing system would be uneconomical and communicatively inefficient. The latter is only possible using a special alphabet designed not for communicative purposes but for the representation of fine-grain phonetic distinctions, such as the International Phonetic Alphabet. Of course, as in all human institutions, ideal phonographic systems do not exist; since they are designed to give permanence to something as dynamic and evanescent as human language, historical residues and conventionalisations are to be expected.

2.7 Phonographic systems have a key advantage for historical linguists: since there is a sound–symbol mapping, it is to be expected that a change in sound has a consequence for the function of the symbol, and thus changes in writing systems give us (in principle) access to the history of sounds.

---

[4] Of course, many speakers of Chinese are bilingual in both Mandarin and Cantonese, something encouraged by the school system; but the general point remains valid.

2.8 To demonstrate this relationship we might take, for instance, a development which took place in the divergence of the English and Frisian sound system from many other varieties of West Germanic, and which had an effect on the evolution, in these dialect areas, of the Germanic writing system known as runes.

2.9 Runes emerged as a distinctive writing system used among the ancient Germanic peoples, possibly through contact with the Mediterranean cultures where various alphabetic systems had earlier appeared (see e.g. Elliott 1959: ch. 1). But the runic alphabet—the futhark—was not stable, and underwent various modifications as the Germanic languages diverged.

2.10 One such modification, unique to English and Frisian runes, was the appearance of two distinctive runes reflecting vowels, viz. ᚩ and ᚠ. (see Page 1973: 20–1). Examination of the two forms indicates their kinship: both derive ultimately from a single form, ᚠ in the Germanic futhark. As West Germanic diverged, a sound change took place in varieties spoken on the North Sea littoral, which included Frisian and the varieties which later developed into Old English. This change is known variously as First Fronting or Anglo-Frisian Brightening/*Aufhellung*. This First Fronting was a shift whereby the original Proto-West Germanic open back vowel /ɑ/ was fronted to /a/; however, there were environments where First Fronting did not take place, and an open back vowel later arose as a separate development from Proto-Germanic *ai*. These developments meant that Anglo-Frisian had two vowels in the open series where Proto-West Germanic had only one. The users of runes responded to these developments by retaining the original rune, ᚠ, for the fronted vowel, but developed a new form, ᚩ, to represent the open back vowel.

2.11 The process involved in the transfer is fairly straightforward, and has been thoroughly discussed by Alfred Bammesberger (1991, esp. p. 397). It seems likely that the reform was triggered by the fact that runes were learned by means of special names; when phonological changes affected these names, changes in the writing system followed (cf. Bammesberger 1991: 395–6). Following Bammesberger, we could develop the following sequence, using the traditional names for the runes as represented in the manuscript tradition:

1. The vowel in Germanic **ask-* would be represented in the older futhark by ᚠ. The vowel in Old English *æsc* (with First Fronting) would quite simply retain the traditional spelling, and thus ᚠ would map onto *æ*.

2. The diphthong in Germanic **aik-* would be represented in the older futhark by ᚠ 1 (16c1). Old English and Old Frisian both monophthongized this vowel to /a:/. The vowel in Old English *āc*, which appears as ᚨ, would be a plausible modification, whereby the second element in the word becomes a 'bind rune' in the futhorc. The result would be that ᚨ would map onto *a* and *ā*.

3. Germanic **ans-* would be represented in the older futhark by the form ᚠ ᛁ ᚺ. The Ingvaeonic change *an-* > *ō-* produced the vowel in Old English *ōs*, which appears as ᚠ. Again, the form ᚠ would plausibly derive from treating ᛁ as a bind rune attached to ᚠ. The result would be that ᚠ would map onto *ō*.

2.12 Such developments are of course more easily catered for in a time before the standardization of writing systems. However, once spelling systems have become fixed they find it harder to respond to changes in the spoken mode, and this difficulty is reflected in the appearance of 'fossil' distinctions (see Lass 1997: 57). Thus, in Present-Day English writing systems, a regular distinction is made between <ee> and <ea> in *meet, meat*; the distinction reflects a difference of pronunciation which is no longer made in standard English accents but which, in the Early Modern English period, was considered prestigious. The <ee>–<ea> distinction is, therefore, in general a fossil, though interestingly some residual distinctions in symbol–sound mapping for these items remain even in standard usages, e.g. *greet, great*.

2.13 An important point here, therefore, is that there is the potential for a temporal lag in the reflection of sound change in the written mode—something to be expected, given the contrast between evanescent speech and (comparatively) permanent writing. This fact has implications for the usefulness of written material; as Patrick Simms-Williams has put it, 'as a general rule, a recording of a phonological innovation in an inscription is significant chronologically, but a *non*-recording is insignificant. Hence epigraphy can rarely stand in the way of *ante*-dating sound changes.' (Simms-Williams 1990: 237)

2.14 The key point to make, though, is that there is a mapping, albeit a complex one, between speech and writing; as stated in 2.0, the two levels of language do, even if in a complex way, map back onto the 'same' language. We must therefore expect a relationship to be developed, and it is no surprise that this relationship involves the notion of the minimal pair, since that notion is to do with perceptual salience.

2.15 Such reflections of sound change in the writing system are of course not invariable. Sometimes the emergence of a new phoneme is not represented in the writing system because a conventionaliza-tion of the writing system has occurred beforehand. A good example of such a conventionalization is represented by the various functions of <c> in Old English. In Pre-Old English the phoneme /k/ had two allophones: [k] in the environment of a following front vowel and [c] in the environment of a following back vowel; the latter, through a process known as 'palatalization', came to be pronounced as [tʃ]. In recorded Old English, both sounds were generally represented by <c>, e.g. *cuman* 'come' (with [k]), *cild* 'child' (with [tʃ]); since [k] and [tʃ] were allophones, such a usage would seem to be expected. However, palatalization did not occur in the environment of front vowels which were the result of a change generally deemed later, namely i-mutation, which produced front vowels in such forms as *cyning* 'king', *cēne* 'bold, keen', *cǣg* 'key'. The appearance in Old English of near-pairs such as *cēn* 'torch' (with initial [tʃ]) and *cēne* 'bold' (with initial [k]) would seem to suggest that [tʃ] and [k] eventually developed as phonemes, once the initial output of i-mutation, a rounded front vowel *ōē, had unrounded to produce ē (in the sequence *ō >*ōē >ē). (See Hogg 1992: 268–9 for further discussion and references.)[5]

---

[5] Why the front vowels which were the outcome of i-mutation did not affect the preceding consonant [k] in the same way as the original front vowels, yielding (e.g.) Present-Day English *ching for king (from Old English *cyning*) is a difficult question; the persistence of [k] in this environment, which seems to be the cause of the phonemicization (Penzl 1969: 104), has not to my knowledge yet been satisfactorily explained.

2.16 However, despite the appearance of pairs of the *cēne, cēn* type, a spelling distinction does not emerge generally in Old English (Hogg 1992: 264–5). A distinction is made only sporadically, with rare occurrences of <k> to represent a presumed /k/ and runic attempts to represent the distinction restricted to a few texts (e.g. the Ruthwell Cross inscription, though this example is problematic; see Hogg 1992: 29 and references there cited). It would seem that the spelling <c> had become conventional in Old English to represent both presumed phonemes; <k> is rare in Romano-British texts, and hence in the insular Celtic uses from which Old English derived its earliest spelling practices. Only in the Middle English period did a spelling distinction <ch, k> arise which resulted, eventually, in the Present-Day distinction represented by the pair *chilled, killed*. The grapheme <c> not followed by diacritic <h>, as a result of the adoption of certain French conventions during the Middle English period, has become used to represent [k] in the environment of <a, o, u> and consonants other than <h>, and [s] in the environment of <e, i, y>, e.g. *cab, cot, cup, certain, city, cyberspace*. (See further the *Oxford English Dictionary* discussion of the letters C, K.)

2.17 Nevertheless, the key point is made: phonological processes have the potential to be reflected in the written record, and therefore writing systems can provide evidence, however carefully it must be judged, for pronunciation.

3 Verse practices

3.0 The second source of evidence for earlier pronunciation has traditionally been based on the analysis of verse: the rhyming, alliterating, and scansion practices adopted by poets (see further Lass 1997: 68ff.). A simple example from the history of English demonstrates the value of this material: rhotic usage in the early nineteenth century.

3.1 It has often been noted that accents of Present-Day English can be categorized as either rhotic or non-rhotic. Rhotic accents 'sound the *r*' in words such as *bar, ford* /bar, fɔrd/; non-rhotic accents do not 'sound the *r*', yielding pronunciations such as /bɑ, fɔd/. In some English-speaking societies, /r/-dropping is stigmatized (e.g. certain urban New York accents); in others, /r/-dropping is a marker of social prestige (British 'Received Pronunciation').

3.2 In England, /r/-dropping seems to be a Late Modern English development, and is witnessed by the appearance of rhymes in verse. Thus the poet John Keats (1795–1821) offers rhymes of the type *thorns*: *fawns*; such a rhyme demonstrates pretty clearly that /r/-dropping was a characteristic of his accent.

3.3 We are fortunate, of course, in knowing a great deal about Keats's social background. Keats was a Londoner, and his place in society, about which he was sensitive, may be roughly categorized as lower middle class. His parents, both of whom died young, ran a coaching inn, while Keats inherited sufficient wealth to allow him to receive a good 'commercial' education, to be apprenticed to a doctor and undergo, by contemporary standards, a fairly advanced course of surgical training (see further Motion 1997: *passim*). Keats had a wide circle of friends and acquaintances with similar backgrounds, and it seems likely that /r/-dropping was a characteristic of their usage as well.

3.4 However, there is evidence that the social circle represented by Keats was not alone in /r/-dropping. It is also displayed in the rhymes of Keats's contemporary, Percy Bysshe Shelley (1792–1822), and Shelley's 'gentlemanly' origins—he was the son of a baronet, and was educated at Eton and Oxford—were often noted by those who met him even when they deprecated his somewhat shocking morals (see Holmes 1974: *passim*). It would seem, therefore, that Keats's rhyming practice provides us with good evidence for the loss of /r/ at the beginning of the nineteenth century (see further Mugglestone 1991; Smith 1996: ch. 2).

3.5 But it is important to be aware of the limitations of the evidence derived from verse. In another context, Eric Stanley has drawn attention to traditional comment on the difficulty of finding rhymes in English and the consequent licence which poets seem to have claimed for 'near-rhymes' such as assonance and consonance: 'I dare almost affirm, that the Difficulty of finding Rhymes, has been the unlucky Cause that has frequently reduc'd even the best of our Poets to take up with Rhymes that have scarce any Consonance, or Agreement in Sound' (Edward Bysshe, *Art of English Poetry* (1702), cited in Stanley 1972: vi). Bysshe is writing at a time when, because of sound changes in previous centuries of which scholars in his own time were generally unaware, the works of earlier poets such as Chaucer or Shakespeare would have seemed to present evidence of lack of 'Agreement in Sound'. But the point is made. The quotation reminds us that we draw conclusions from the evidence supplied by rhyme based on certain assumptions which are at least arguable— namely, that poets always attempted true rhyme, and that verse always reflects the rhythms of non-literary speech.

3.6 It is possible to be both over-optimistic and over-sceptical about the evidence supplied by verse. We know for a fact, from other evidence, that (for instance) in the eighteenth century rhymes of the *sea*: *say* type were, in many accents of English, 'conventional', that is, accepted as rhymes in literary verse not because they were true ear-rhymes but because they were sanctioned by tradition; there is good evidence that they had been true ear rhymes in many accents in the past. Further, eye-rhymes of the *rough*: *bough* type were, we know, accepted by a literate community whose primary encounter with verse was to do with reading silently rather than listening to an oral performance. Such restrictions apply even to earlier stages of verse, though, where a spoken performance might be regarded as more prototypical in its social functioning. Medieval English writers from the end of the fourteenth century, for instance, commonly rhyme pairs such as *Rome* : *to me*, where *Rome* is a trochaic unit with stress on the first syllable but where it is hard to argue that the phrase *to me* is anything other than an iamb, with stress on the second syllable (see, for example, John Gower, *Confessio Amantis*, III: 99–100, in Macaulay 1900: 229). The usage seems to us now both peculiar and forced, but it occurs frequently enough in English high-status art poetry of the late fourteenth century to indicate that it was not only acceptable but just possibly regarded as elegant.

3.7 And there is indeed some evidence that /r/-dropping was not seen as universally acceptable in Keats's time. This fact was demonstrated rather cruelly in some of the reviews of his poetry which Keats received, and which, it is usually claimed, caused him considerable distress. Thus John Lockhart, in the *Edinburgh Review*, criticized Keats in the following terms: he was 'without learning enough to distinguish between the written language of Englishmen and the spoken jargon of Cockneys' (Mugglestone 1991: 59); and one point of criticism singled out by Lockhart for attack was Keats's apparent non-rhoticity displayed in his rhyming practice. Lockhart was of course a Scot, whose native speech would have been rhotic, and thus it could be argued that his criticism was based on the coincidence of his own speech and the conventional presence of <r> in contemporary (and present-day) English writing. Perhaps more salient are the comments of later poets, such as Thomas Hood the younger, who referred as late as 1877 to 'such atrocities as "morn" and "dawn", . . . "fought" and "sort" 'as 'fatal to the success of verse' (cited in Mugglestone 1991: 60).

3.8 But to move from such reservations to wholesale scepticism about the value of rhyming evidence, as some have done, is too extreme. Most verse, even now, does bear a close relationship to speech, and, given the paucity of evidence available for many periods in the history of English it seems perverse simply to ignore a whole category of evidence. The proper response would seem to be to use verse evidence, but to do so alongside other sources. It is to such another source, contemporary comments on pronunciation, that we might now turn.

4 Contemporary comments

4.0 It may be observed that evidence for /r/-loss in Late Modern English is supplied not just by verse but also by contemporary observers of language. B. H. Smart, for instance, in his prescriptivist *A Grammar of English Sounds* (1812), comments that 'the smooth R, is often pronounced with so little force, as to be, in fact, nothing more than the vowel sound AH' (cited in Mugglestone 1991: 61; 'smooth *R*' in Smart's usage seems to be the realization of /r/ in postvocalic and final positions, as opposed to initial 'rough *R*'). Although in his earlier *A Practical Grammar of English Pronunciation* (1810) Smart seems to have regarded non-rhoticity as something Londoners were 'too liable' to exhibit, he nevertheless seems to accept it as characteristic of the speech of significant numbers of persons whose social status is not in doubt. Thus Smart's evidence may be seen as a valuable complement to the evidence supplied by contemporary poets.

4.1 The English language has attracted contemporary comment for much of its history, since the end of the Old English period when Ælfric, in his *Grammar* (*c*.1000), offered helpful parallels between Latin (the principal object of his attention) and his own native vernacular. And during the Middle English period we are lucky to have comments on such matters as rhetorical practice (as by Geoffrey Chaucer) and on dialectal variation (as by John Trevisa and William Caxton). But scholarly work on English in the modern sense really begins during the Early Modern period, as the English language, hitherto a (comparatively) despised vernacular, came, as the result of interplay between Renaissance, Reformation, and the rise of a vernacular-speaking bourgeoisie, to be regarded as an object worthy of learned attention (see further Smith 2006 and references there cited).

4.2 Many of these earlier scholars were highly intelligent and perceptive individuals, and their evidence has to be taken as a serious contribution to the history of the language. To demonstrate the usefulness of the evidence they supply, we will look at a comparatively simple example: the interpretation of <gh>-spellings in the seventeenth and eighteenth centuries.

4.3 In Present-Day English, <gh>-spellings have a number of functions:

a. they can be 'silent', as in *daughter, though, bought, straight, height, weigh, high, night*. In these cases, <gh> can have a diacritic function comparable to final <e>; cf. the modern jocular misspellings *nite* for *night*, *lite* for *light*.

b. they can map onto /f/, as in *tough, laugh, draught, laughter.*
c. they can be used to represent /g/ in *ghost, aghast, ghastly,* although interestingly the use of <gh> for /g/ seems to have a semantic implication, in that words where it appears generally have to do with the notions fear, shock, etc.

4.4 It will be clear, therefore, that there are a series of mappings between symbol and sound: to use the ancient and medieval terminology referred to earlier in this chapter, the 'figure' (*figura*) <gh> maps onto a variety of 'powers' (*potestates* = sound equivalents), viz. zero, /f/, /g/.

4.5 In origin, the figure <gh> seems to have mapped onto the power /x/, emerging in the Early Middle English period as one of the replacements for Old English <h>. <h> was used in Old French as a diacritic mark (Pope 1934: 277, 288), 'juxtaposed to a letter to indicate simply that its pronunciation was not what would normally be expected under the conditions in which it stood' (Pope 1934: 277), and this pattern seems to have been transferred to English after the Norman Conquest, generating <ch, th> etc. The Middle English sound equivalent of <gh> was therefore /x/.

4.6 The Present-Day English pattern seems to have emerged during the course of the fifteenth and sixteenth centuries, and here an examination of the various forms of primary evidence becomes invaluable. For the silencing of <gh> in 'high' etc., evidence begins to appear in late Middle English, as witnessed by spellings such as *hie.* Silent <gh> is similarly indicated by the appearance of 'back-spellings', such as *wright* for 'write'. (For examples, see McIntosh, Samuels and Benskin 1986: vol. iv.)

4.7 For the development to /f/, spellings such as *thorf* in the fifteenth-century *Paston Letters* are indicative. The /ft/ in *laughter* seems to have emerged at much the same time, though interestingly, there are Early Modern English records of forms with /ft/ which have not survived into Present-Day English, such as *dafter* 'daughter', *soft* 'sought'. The form *thof* 'though', appearing as a 'vulgarism' in Fielding's *Tom Jones*, predates Early Modern English, being recorded widely in Northern Middle English. (See Wyld 1936: 288.)

4.8 The mapping <gh> /g/ is described by the *Oxford English Dictionary* as 'a mere capricious substitute for *g*'; Caxton has spellings such as *ghoos, ghoot, gherle* for Present-Day English *goose, goat, girl* but the modern usage, interestingly, is generally found in initial position in words belonging to a particular semantic field: *ghost, ghoul, ghastly, aghast* (but cf. *ghazi, ghetto, gherkin, ghee*, which are loanwords used in rather specialist contexts). It would seem that <gh> with this sound value has, during the Modern English period, developed a particular semantic correlation: an interesting correlation, somewhat comparable with phonaesthesia, which could only develop in conditions of widespread literacy.

4.9 This pattern did not emerge in a straightforward way, however, and here the evidence of contemporary commentators is of interest. Two such commentators, both of them excellent observers of contemporary language, might be taken as examples: Christopher Cooper and Sylvester Douglas.

4.10 Cooper was a schoolmaster at Bishop's Stortford, a small town in rural Hertfordshire, at the end of the seventeenth century. Although he dedicated the first version of his grammar to an eminent contemporary savant (Seth Ward, mathematician, Bishop of Salisbury and an early member of the Royal Society), his writings on language made little impact in his time. Cooper was more interested in the practicalities of language description and instruction than in the philosophising on linguistic universals which attracted widespread contemporary attention and comment. However, he is now considered the greatest of seventeenth-century English phoneticians (Dobson 1968: 280). His *Grammar* appeared in two versions: in Latin (*Grammatica Linguae Anglicanae*, 1685), and in English (*The English Teacher*, 1687).

4.11 Cooper's discussion of <gh> is characteristically precise:

Hodie apud nos desuevit pronunciatio *gh*, retinetur tamen in scriptura; ut *Alight* resido, *almighty* omnipotens...*Gh* in *cough* tussio, *laugh* tussio... pronunciatur ut *f.* (Jones 1912: 67–8)

In a later paragraph dealing with homophones, he notes that *ghost* 'spiritus' is differentiated by spelling but not pronunciation from *go'st* 'vadis' (Jones 1912: 78), which suggests that he saw the *gh* spelling as to do with meaning-differentiation.

4.12 However, there are some interesting further comments. First, Cooper shows throughout his book an awareness of spelling variation, so for the gloss 'pagus' he offers '*burrough* vel *burrow*', while for 'per' he offers '*thorough* vel *thorow*' (cf. Present-Day English *through*). Even more interesting is the way in which he deals with the ancestor of Present-Day English *enough*. Cooper states that *gh* in *enough* 'quantitatem denotans, pronunciatur ut *f. Enough* numerum denotans sonatur (et melius scriberetur) *enow*' (Jones 1912: 68). In other words, he identifies two pronunciations for Present-Day English *enough* which are semantically differentiated. Historically, of course, this differentiation is explicable; *enow* derives from an inflected form of Old English *genōg*, while *enough* derives from an uninflected form (see Jordan 1974: 132, para. 125). The distinction is widespread in Middle English, and also in Older Scots, where *eneuch/enew* are distributed depending on the nature of the noun being modified or qualified. In Older Scots, *eneuch* is used to modify a mass noun while *enew* is used to modify a count noun (see Macafee 2002: cxi). Interestingly, the form *enow* is recorded as modifying the plural nouns *teats*, *paps* in mid-twentieth-century English dialects (see Upton *et al.* 1994: 485).

4.13 Sylvester Douglas lived a century later than Cooper. Douglas was a characteristic product of the Scottish Enlightenment. Born in 1744 in rural Aberdeenshire, he was educated at the Universities of Aberdeen and Leiden in the Netherlands; in the 1790s he developed a political career in Ireland around the period of the Act of Union between Britain and Ireland (1801), and later in London. He married the daughter of an earlier Prime Minister, Lord North, and was elevated to the peerage in 1800, as Lord Glenbervie.

4.14 Douglas has been described, on the evidence of his surviving personal writings, as a 'serious and perhaps even slightly pedantic individual' (Jones 1991: 2), 'certainly no genius [but] ... in many respects a notable man' (Sichel 1910: 1–5, cited in Jones 1991: 3). He never fulfilled his ambitions as a writer, publishing comparatively little in his lifetime other than short articles on Hungarian wines and Scottish peat moss; he also composed a translation of an Italian poem with a thoughtful introduction which was printed (but unpublished) by John Murray in 1822. Douglas's *Treatise on the Provincial Dialect of Scotland* survives in two manuscript versions, the first in his own hand and the second probably in the hand of one of his clerks but with corrections by the author. The second version has the inscription 'S. Douglas, Lincoln's Inn, 1779' on the flyleaf, in the clerk's hand. On the evidence of the *Treatise*, Douglas was, it seems, an accurate observer of contemporary educated usage and indeed a linguistic theorist of some ability (see Jones 1991: ix).

4.15 Douglas's comments on *gh* are worth quoting; they fall under his discussion of the letter *g*.

The Germans and Dutch make the *g* a guttural semivowel, analogous to their *ch*, but softer in the same proportion as our hard *g* is softer than *k*. One would expect to find this softer guttural in the Scotch [*sic*] manner of pronouncing *gh* in *light, thought, sight*, but I cannot, by my ear, discover any difference between the Scotch *ch*, and *gh*. ... *Gh*, and *gu* at the beginning of words have the sound of the hard *g*, as *ghost, guest, guardian*. In the middle of words *gh* is mute, as in *sight, sought*, and, often, at the end; as *plough, bough, though*. Sometimes at the end *gh* has the sound of *f*, as *rough, cough, laugh* and in the middle, as in the word *laughter*. It is a provincial pronunciation in some countries of the west of England to say *oft*, and *thoft*, for *ought* and *thought*. I know one instance of a man of education and eminence in a learned profession who retains this mode of sounding those words. The Scotch name the *g* like the English word *jay*. The English name rhymes to *bee.*'   (Jones 1991: 127)

4.16 Douglas's account, annoyingly, does not give us his pronunciation of *enough* with [f], but he does record *enow*, rhyming it with *how, now, allow, brow* etc., and also (interestingly) '*low* (as a cow), *mow* (of barley or corn of any sort), ... *sow (sus)*' (Jones 1991: 177); the gloss *sus* indicates that *sow* here is not Present-Day English *sow* but the rarer word *sough*.

4.17 Douglas's terminology may be conventional—his references to 'letter', 'name' etc. clearly derive from the ancient doctrine of *littera* (see 2.1), but he gives us invaluable information about the kind of variant pronunciations which existed in educated speech towards the end of the eighteenth century. But of course his value, like that of Cooper, needs to be judged by careful comparison with other sources of evidence: Douglas's discussion of the pronunciations in [f], for instance, of *thought, ought* can be placed alongside those conventional spellings recorded in Early Modern English (see 4.7).

5 Reconstruction

5.0 There remains a further source of information for linguistic historians, but whereas the sources described hitherto make direct reference to texts, this source is indirect: linguistic reconstruction.

5.1 As is well known, linguistic reconstruction was developed in the nineteenth century for the purposes of establishing genetic relationships between languages and for recovering their prehistory; the method was related to other philological practices, such as classical textual criticism, as well as evolutionary biology, and may well have inspired Darwin. It was essentially an Enlightenment phenomenon, though with roots in the Renaissance; Roger Lass has drawn attention to the work of Conrad Gestner (*Mithridates*, 1555), who noted the existence of 'mother' languages and used the term *cognatae* to refer to groups of related languages (see Lass 1997: 107–8, and also 5.4, below). The most famous figure for Indo-Europeanists, though, is Sir William Jones (1746–94), who noticed the similarities between such languages as Sanskrit, Latin, and English, and postulated the existence of a common ancestor which had not been recorded; reconstruction was a means by which the essential linguistic characteristics of this ancestor could be worked out. Reconstruction enabled scholars to supplement the evidence supplied by the (frequently) fragmentary pieces of primary sources with a rather more comprehensive account of early language states.

5.2 It is usual to distinguish two kinds of reconstruction: comparative and internal. Comparative reconstruction proceeds, as its name suggests, through the comparison of distinct languages, or varieties of the same language, in order to work out the structure of the common ancestor language or variety. Internal reconstruction operates through the analysis of paradigmatic variation within a single language or variety.

5.3 The two procedures are complementary, and can be illustrated from the history of English and related Germanic dialects. In Old English, the verb *cēosan* 'choose' (infinitive) has the following principal parts: *ceas* (third-person preterite singular), *curon* (preterite plural), (*ge*)*coren* (past participle). As is suggested by the Present-Day English pronunciation, *c* in *cēosan* was pronounced [tʃ] in Old English; however, the evidence also suggests that *c* was pronounced as [k] in *curon*, (*ge*)*coren*.

5.4 Internal reconstruction would suggest that [k] and [tʃ] in these words go back to a common ancestor. The evidence of other items in Old English suggests that this common ancestor was [k], phonemically /k/, and this suggestion is supported if comparative reconstruction is adopted. Old English is closely related to other Germanic languages, such as Old Norse and Gothic, which are regarded as 'cognate' languages (cf. Latin *cognātus* 'born together'). The Old Norse cognate for *cēosan* is *kjōsa*, and the Gothic cognate is *kiusan*, and in both cases the evidence suggests that *k* was pronounced [k]. It thus seems likely that [tʃ] in *cēosan* is an innovation in Old English, derived from an earlier *[k].

5.5 Linguistic reconstruction was one of the great intellectual advances of the nineteenth century, relating to similar paradigmatic shifts in, for example, textual criticism of the Bible and (most spectacularly) the Darwinian insight as to the origin of species, and it has shown its value for historians of the language on numerous occasions. But it is important to be aware of its limitations. The reconstructed form *[k]— more properly in this instance */k/—is an abstraction; we have no historically attested information as to its range of allophonic realizations and thus it is not possible, using reconstruction, to be certain as to what this reconstructed form sounded like, although (of course) we have Present-Day usages as a guide (cf. the important discussion of Saussure's famous 'laryngeals', reconstructed for Hittite, whose phonemic status seems generally, if not universally, established but whose articulatory characteristics are still a matter for considerable scholarly dispute). Reconstruction enables scholars to envisage systems in the past; it does not enable scholars to speak that language. As Antoine Meillet put it, 'La grammaire comparée n'a pas pour but de reconstruire l'indo-européen' (Meillet 1937: viii); Roger Lass makes a rather similar point when he points out that a 'protolanguage is an "idealization" or "abstraction" ' albeit 'paradoxically, a concrete one' (1997: 273; Lass's discussion of reconstruction is an important theoretical survey). The choice of phonological or phonetic symbol to represent such abstractions is consequently at one level rather arbitrary.

5.6 Moreover, the whole process of reconstruction depends on the adoption of a particular model of linguistic evolution: the so-called 'tree model', whereby cognate languages and forms descend from a common ancestor. The tree model is, once more, a nineteenth-century invention, clearly relating to the phylogenetic tree developed by the proponents of biological evolution in order to illustrate the divergence of species. However, linguistic evolution differs from biological evolution in that languages and varieties can acquire and transmit characteristics through contact with other languages and varieties, such as so-called 'borrowing' of vocabulary; and this fact makes the tree model problematic. Nineteenth-century scholars were well aware of this difficulty, and developed a supplementary 'wave model' to accommodate the phenomenon of contact. These models are still very much current, and continue to be refined (see Lass 1997: 143–57).

5.7 More recently, various attempts have been made to renew this connection between evolutionary phylogenetics and linguistic reconstruction (see the essays in Forster and Renfrew 2006). However, these approaches have met with some criticism; as Heggarty has pointed out (2006: 193–4):

however applicable and promising phylogenetic methods might appear to be at first sight as tools for investigating language histories, even a cursory look at how language behaves in reality shows just how problematic their application to language data can be ... The facets of language that we have looked at here, and more generally its inherent susceptibility to being moulded by external socio-cultural forces, conspire to make the attempt to use language data to extrapolate back into the unknown past an enterprise fraught with pitfalls.

5.8 It could be argued therefore that—given its limitations—reconstruction should be dismissed by historical linguists, on the grounds of imprecision. Such an argument would be quite wrong. As was discussed in Chapter 1, most historians have always recognized that their interpretations of the past are necessarily partial, incomplete, provisional, but, equally, most historians hold that this recognition is not disabling. Rather, they hold that the interpretative exercise is a continuing one, and that the tools to be used for such interpretations, provided that the limitations of those tools are understood, remain valid; the best (i.e. the most precise) should not be seen as the enemy of the good (i.e. the adequately precise). The same goes for linguistic historiography; the difficulty (and it is important to be aware of this) is to decide what is meant by adequacy in this context. We cannot, as has rightly been argued, afford 'stabs in the dark' (McMahon and McMahon 2006: 160); but bringing socio-cultural and linguistic knowledge into articulation should, it may be hoped, make our use of reconstructive techniques more legitimate.

5.9 It is worth in this context recalling that our knowledge of the past is always in some sense partial; just because we know a lot more about (say) the Victorian era, because of the availability of primary sources, than (say) the Babylonian era does not mean that we know everything about the former. Reconstructive techniques thus retain their value even when dealing with periods for which the amount of surviving information is quite considerable.

5.10 Reconstruction of course underpins the standard terminology adopted for the classification of language states, notably the distinction between *proto-* and *pre-* languages. Thus it is traditional to label the presumed common ancestor of all the recorded Germanic languages (English, German, Dutch, Gothic, Danish, Swedish, Norwegian, Afrikaans, etc.) as Proto-Germanic, sometimes referred to as Primitive Germanic. Modern scholars are sometimes reluctant to adopt the usage of *primitive*, probably because of the word's potentially problematic connotations of social unsophistication. For this reason (except in quotations) the term *primitive* will not be used in this book; rather, the term *proto-* will be used. (This usage corresponds to the prefix *ur-* used in German, e.g. *Urgermanisch.*)

5.11 The term *proto-* is central to reconstruction, signifying a nodal point on a tree model of linguistic relationships. The term should be carefully distinguished from another usage, *pre-* as in 'Pre-Germanic', 'Pre-Old English'. In some scholarly traditions, *pre-* is used to refer to the period in a language before written records; thus 'Pre-Old English' is, for some scholars, Old English of the period between the divergence of English from the other Germanic dialects to become a language but before written manifestations appear.

5.12 This use for the term *pre-* is not adopted in this book; such a practice would seem to suggest a clear-cut moment of divergence between language states, when an argument of this book is that such clear-cut divergences are not to be had. Rather, when periods before written records are discussed, they will be referred to as *prehistoric*. The prefix *pre-* is retained instead to refer to the period of divergence, as a variety develops such differences from its 'parent' and 'sisters' as to form a distinct language (i.e. it refers to the *line* in a tree diagram). 'Pre-Old English', therefore, is taken here to refer to the period between the node 'Anglo-Frisian' and the node 'Old English', the latter including a prehistoric period. Prehistoric Old English is thus the earliest period in the history of the language when it is possible to refer to English as a language distinct from the other varieties of Germanic. The distinction between *pre-* and *prehistoric*

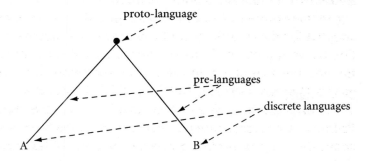

Prehistoric A, B = before written records
Historic A, B = from the appearance of written records

FIGURE 2.1 The relationship between proto-, pre-, and prehistoric language states

may seem to be rather technical and (to some) unnecessary, but it is nevertheless, it is argued here, important; it is a theme of this book, already raised in Chapter 1, that language change is an emergent process, and we therefore need a way of referring to the process of divergence, as one variety diverges from another. A schematic representation of the relationships between *proto-*, *pre-*, and *prehistoric* language states appears as Figure 2.1, though it is important to realize that such schematizations are themselves problematic, a freeze-frame pictorial representation which attempts to capture movement in fixed form.

6 The question 'why?'

6.0 Reconstruction and the interpretation of primary evidence are the basic tools of the historical linguist. With all necessary caveats about their limitations, these tools enable us to offer a conspectus of the kinds of pronunciation to be found in past periods of the language.

6.1 These tools, therefore, allow us to answer, to a greater or lesser extent, the question 'what?', and for many historians of the language answers to this question are sufficient. But, as was discussed in Chapter 1, historians are also interested in other questions, such as 'why?', and the question 'why?' is the concern of the remainder of this book.

3

Phonological Approaches and Processes

1 Splits, mergers, and shifts

1.0 In Chapter 1, various kinds of sound change were identified: splits, mergers, and shifts. These processes will be referred to repeatedly in what follows, so they need some further unpacking here.

1.1 Arguably the most straightforward kind of sound change is that known as *split*. In taxonomic terms, splits may be quite simply defined: they occur when two allophones of a single phoneme become separate phonemes, as demonstrated by the existence of a contrastive minimal pair. Thus in Old English the phoneme /f/ had two allophones, [f] and [v], which were in complementary distribution within the lexicon. [f] appeared word-initially and -finally, as in *fela*, *hlāf*; [v] appeared medially, as in *hlāford*. However, during the Middle English period, minimal pairs of the kind *fine* : *vine*, *proof* : *prove* appeared, whereby the change from one sound to another causes the meaning of the form in question to change; thus the sounds [f] and [v] are in contrastive position, and are therefore separate phonemes—namely, /f, v/.

1.2 The written mode responded rather slowly to these developments, and it is noticeable that the Present-Day English writing system continues to have problems with these fricatives. Only the /v, f/ distinction seems to be fairly well reflected in the Present-Day English writing system, though even there uncertainties exist over

such pairs as *dwarfs, dwarves*. There is some early evidence for a
<v>-grapheme in Old English, presumably, given the context,
reflecting a voiced sound. However, such examples are sporadic in
the surviving written record. Helmut Gneuss (1994: 58) reports the
form *uers* for 'verse' in some Old English glosses, and also significant
may be the appearance of the form *hliuade* 'towered' in MS London,
British Library, Cotton Vitellius A.xv (the Beowulf Manuscript; cf.
the usual Old English form *hlifian*). Otherwise the appearance of the
<v>-grapheme is a Middle English phenomenon, with allographs
≪v≫ and ≪u≫ depending on context (≪v≫ is usual in
initial position, while ≪u≫ appears in medial position). However,
the distinction is not marked in the orthography of *The Ormulum*,
which dates from *c*.1200 (cf. *wif, wifess*), suggesting that the distinction was not yet phonemic in the variety represented by that important text.

1.3 A second kind of sound change is a *merger*, whereby phonemic distinctions are lost. A good example is the /w/ : /ʍ/ distinction, which still survives in some varieties of Scots and Scottish
English and is occasionally restored in prestigious accents under
the influence of spelling. In Old English, the two sounds were
carefully distinguished in the writing system, with <hw> for /ʍ/
and <w> for /w/, as in *hwæl* 'whale', *wæl* 'slaughter'. However, in
many accents of Present-Day English the distinction has been lost,
so that pairs such as *what, watt* are homophones. Again, the process
seems to have been an ongoing one, beginning in southern accents
of Middle English and represented in the written form by back-
spellings such as *where* for 'were'. In prestigious accents in the Early
Modern period the distinction was retained, but there is good
evidence that merger was already under way in 'vulgar' speech, as
witnessed by homophone lists from the seventeenth century such as
that which appears in Elisha Coles's *The Compleat English Schoolmaster* (1674). By the eighteenth century the merger seems to have
been general in prestigious use (see Wyld 1936: 312); it is recorded,
for instance, by James Elphinston in his *The Principles of the
English Language, or English Grammar* (1765). Elphinston deplores

the usage, but this may be because, like many eighteenth-century commentators, he was Scottish (see Lawson 1998, cited in Stuart-Smith 1999).

1.4 Finally, there are *shifts*, whereby sounds are redistributed in the lexicon. A good example of a shift is Grimm's Law, otherwise known as the First Consonant Shift (to distinguish it from the Second, or High German, Consonant Shift). Grimm's Law is a phenomenon which distinguishes the Germanic from the other Indo-European languages; it is usually (though not invariably) seen as a Germanic innovation. The classical account of Grimm's Law runs something as follows: except in certain contexts, Proto-Indo-European /b, d, g/ are reflected in Proto-Germanic as /p, t, k/, respectively; Proto-Indo-European /p, t, k/ are reflected in Proto-Germanic as /f, θ, x/; Proto-Indo-European /bh, dh, gh/ (i.e. phonemic plosives with aspiration) are reflected in Proto-Germanic as /b, d, g/. (The exceptions to this development, first coherently discussed by the Neogrammarian linguist Karl Verner, are the result of some specific environments, to do with stress patterns.) A simplified diagram illustrating the development appears as Figure 3.1 (after Bynon 1977: 83).

Pre-Germanic

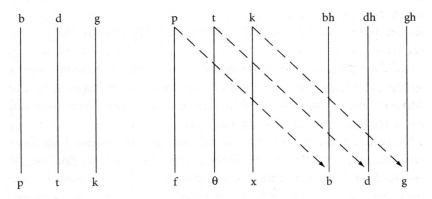

Proto-Germanic
(See Bynon 1977: 83 for a more detailed outline).

FIGURE 3.1 Grimm's Law. The dotted lines represent the operation of Verner's Law

1.5 As well as 'simple' splits, mergers and shifts, there are sound changes which bring these elements together. Split and merger, for instance, are both involved, it will be argued in Chapter 6, in the operation of the Great Vowel Shift.

1.6 The processes which result in splits, mergers, and shifts are of course gradual ones; variations can exist in a language for some time without a change resulting. As Roger Lass puts it, 'stable variation is one of the common states for language' (1997: 304). Old English possessed voiced as well as voiceless fricatives, but they were in complementary, not contrastive, distribution. The merger whereby the /ʍ/ : /w/ distinction was lost seems to have been the result of a long-term process of '/h/-loss' in the history of English, which affected medial and final /h/ first and only subsequently initial /h/ (see Lutz 1991). The development which gave rise to Grimm's Law seems to depend on the existence of aspirated allophones of /p t,k/, which were reinterpreted as fricatives by those who encountered them; we will be returning to this example at the end of this chapter.

1.7 Sound change, therefore, depends on the fourth category identified by John Wells and discussed in Chapter 1: realizational and phonotactic differences, which can be 'activated' phonologically at any point in time when the conditions are right.

2 Sound change as an emergent phenomenon

2.0 The emergence of minimal pairs is, then, a gradual, not a sudden, process, and to illustrate this we might investigate the history of a sound whose phonemic status remains controversial for English, namely, the velar nasal [ŋ].

2.1 The sound [ŋ] appears in all varieties of Present-Day English, but its phonemic status varies. In Southern British English /ŋ/ is generally perceived as a distinct phoneme, as witnessed by the minimal pair *sin*, *sing*, where the graphemic cluster <ng> represents a single phonological segment, in the same way as <sh> represents the single segment /ʃ/. This process is known as 'ŋ Coalescence' (Wells 1982: 188–9). However, [ŋ] is not phonemic in many varieties of Northern and Western British English, where it is an allophone of /n/ in the environment of a following /g/. There are also some interesting paradigmatic alternations: in Southern British English /ŋ/ appears finally in *strong*, but compare the comparative adjective *stronger* /strɔŋgə/, beside generalized /ŋ/ in *bang* 'loud noise', *banger* 'sausage', 'decrepit motor vehicle' (slang).

2.2 [ŋ] is a problematic sound in the history of English. It is worth noting that it was regularly represented by a distinct rune in both the Germanic futhark and the Old English futhorc (see Page 1973: 47 and *passim*), which—if it is accepted that the runemasters were attempting a mapping between phoneme and grapheme—suggests that it may have been perceived as a distinct phoneme even at this early date in the history of English. (It may be of interest to note that, in the Germanic futhark, the rune for 'ŋ' is generally physically smaller than other runes, suggesting that its status was perceived as in some senses problematic, and it was expanded to make its size equivalent to other runes only in the Old English futhorc; cf. Germanic ◇ beside Old English ᛝ.)

2.3 However, a distinct letter form for /ŋ/ was not sustained, and most authorities are of the opinion that [ŋ] was in Old English an allophone, i.e. a contextual variant of /n/, found in the environment of a following /g/ (see Hogg 1992: 39). It is generally held that the phoneme /ŋ/ emerged only in the early seventeenth century, when it was recognized as a distinct sound by orthoepists and phoneticians such as Robert Robinson and Alexander Gil (see Dobson 1968: 953). To avoid the creation of a new letter altogether, the spelling cluster <ng> was then reinterpreted as the appropriate written-language representation for the new phoneme /ŋ/.[6]

---

[6] An interesting alternative development, still recorded in many accents, is for [n] to appear in place of [ŋ] in final position, with varying sociolinguistic significance; compare, for example, stereotypical 'upper-class' *huntin', shootin', fishin'* with stereotypical 'lower-class' *nuffin'* 'nothing'. The usage is recorded by Christopher Cooper in 1687, who, in his list of words 'that have the same pronunciation, but differing signification and manner of writing', offers the pair *coffin : coughing*. See further Lass (1997: 75n).

2.4 It is worth recalling, though, that the early phoneticians were generally concerned with recording—and establishing appropriate writing systems to reflect—careful speech which they deemed to be prestigious. It seems quite likely that, throughout the history of English, the phonemic status of [ŋ] varied diatopically and stylistically, much as it does in Present-Day English varieties.

2.5 What this example demonstrates is that the story of /ŋ/ is a more complex one than might at first seem the case. We may wish to date this particular split to the early seventeenth century on evidential grounds, but the [ŋ]-sound seems to have existed long before then, as a variant produced by the phonetic process known as assimilation. This phonemicization would seem to be the outcome of a long process of dynamic competition between phonetically derived variants. The phonemicization of /ŋ/ was potentially available throughout, it would seem, the history of English, but emerged (and thus became salient in semantic terms) only in certain times and places.

2.6 Since it has a systemic implication, though one with distinct diachronic and diatopic distributions, the [ŋ] > /ŋ/ development would therefore seem to be a real sound change in terms of our working definition: *a sound change has taken place when a variant form, mechanically produced, is imitated by a second person and that process of imitation causes the system of the imitating individual to change.*

2.7 However, questions of explanation remain. Why did the change [ŋ] > /ŋ/ happen when and where it did? Is it possible, moreover, to explain the current diatopic and stylistic distribution of the /ŋ/-phoneme, and to explain why the phonemicization in some accents took place at a given point in time but did not in others?

2.8 According to most authorities, the development seems to be largely mechanical, the outcome of changes elsewhere in the system which resulted fortuitously in the appearance of relevant minimal pairs. In the case of [ŋ] > /ŋ/, assimilation of velar plosive [g] to velar nasal [ŋ] is always a plausible phonetic development, and it seems that phonemicization was possible at any point in time. Thus the development of /ŋ/ as a distinct phoneme in the sixteenth century in some accents is essentially a chance event which was sustained through the monitoring process.

3 Explaining split: voiced and voiceless fricatives

3.0 Of course, some splits can be explained more precisely, and here we might look again at the phonemicization of the voiced–voiceless distinction in the English fricatives. It is conventional to describe Present-Day English as having three sets of fricative, each consisting of voiced and voiceless phonemes:

/f, v/
/s, z/
/θ, ð/

In each case there are Present-Day English minimal pairs to illustrate the phonemic character of the voiced–voiceless distinction: *vine* and *fine, house* (noun) and *house* (verb), *thy* and *thigh.*

3.1 It is noticeable, though, that the Present-Day English writing system continues to have problems with these fricatives. Early evidence for such representation is limited (see 1.2, above). Otherwise the appearance of the <v>-grapheme is a Middle English phenomenon, with allographs ≪v≫ and ≪u≫ depending on context (see Chapter 2, 2.2).

3.2 <th>, derived from the Latin usage which itself mapped onto Greek, was used in the earliest Old English to represent [θ, ð]. However, this usage was not sustained, and <th> was subsequently replaced in Old English texts by the letters þ 'thorn', ð 'eth'. Eth appears in texts from *c.*700 AD onwards, with thorn, in origin a runic letter, being transferred to non-runic scripts slightly later. There is some evidence that these two letters were used for a while to represent voiced and voiceless sounds, respectively, even though there was no phonemic distinction in Old English. However, this practice did not persist, and the two soon became interchangeable.

3.3 <th> is used in Present-Day English for both /θ, ð/, though an alternative spelling, <dh>, would seem to be a fairly obvious extrapolation. The spelling <dh> was used to represent the voiced sound by a number of orthoepists, but has not been adopted in modern English spelling systems except in specialist or philologically informed writings; compare Tolkien's use of <dh> in *The Lord of the Rings* in the place-name *Caradhras*, or its use to represent /ð/ in specialist borrowed vocabulary, such as *sandhi*.

3.4 It has been argued that the failure to develop an accepted graphemic distinction to reflect the voiced–voiceless distinction of /θ, ð/ is related to the paucity of minimal pairs distinguishing these phonemes. It is noticeable that, for instance, /ð/ appears in initial position in Present-Day English prestige accents only in closed-class words such as determiners and pronouns, giving rise to only a few, rather obscure minimal pairs (e.g. *thy : thigh*). Many late Middle English varieties did retain the grapheme <þ> in initial position in such words, and this practice continued into Early Modern English where <þ> was replaced by <y>, as in <ye> 'the', <yt> 'that'. However, the practice was not sustained beyond the seventeenth century in printed books, though lasting in informal writings well into the nineteenth century. It is possible that this written practice was adopted to reflect the /θ, ð/ distinction, but it is equally possible that it was simply a conventional abbreviation.

3.5 <s, z> seem to be interchangeable in many situations, with the choice of one rather than another seemingly cultural rather than linguistically conditioned (cf. British–US distinctions between *criticise* and *criticize*). Indeed, the letter <z> in general, however it was precisely realized in writing, seems to have had a marginal status in most (though not all) languages which used and use a Latin-derived alphabet. The late Anglo-Saxon writer Ælfric perceived its restricted range when he described it in his *Grammar* thus: *se staef is genumen of Grecum to ledenspraece for greciscum wordum* (Zupitza 1880: 6). Ælfric's comment, which was included in a textbook for the teaching of Latin, seems to have been an accurate summary of the situation in Latin scripts since antiquity.

3.6 When <z> was transferred to English, the evidence is that, there too, it was only employed as a specialized and learned letter. In Old English its use seems to have been generally restricted to what the *Oxford English Dictionary* rather quaintly refers to as 'alien' words, such as personal names (e.g. *Zefferus* 'Zephyrus', *Baldazar*), with the phonetic correlate [ts], indicated by its sporadic use in place of <ts> in for instance *bezt* 'best' beside more common *betst* (Campbell 1959: 22; Hogg 1992: 37). In Old English scripts, <z> seems to have been realized (albeit somewhat floridly as befits a rarity) in its 'figure-2' ≪z≫-form (see e.g. the form in the name *Azarias* in *The Exeter Book*, fol. 53a, in Chambers *et al.* 1933). During the Middle English and Early Modern English periods, <z> was realized in handwriting both as ≪z≫ (with or without crossbar) and as ≪3≫; the latter survives in some varieties of present-day handwriting, while the former is the usual form in print. However it was realized, <z> was regarded as an optional rather than a necessary part of the English spelling system. When in Shakespeare's *King Lear* one character insults another by calling him *thou whoreson zed, thou unnecessary letter*, contemporary audiences would have appreciated the point being made about the redundancy of the form— a reference which would have been peculiarly apt at a time when spelling reform was high on the intellectual agenda.

3.7 The graphemic evidence for the phonemicization of voiced and voiceless fricatives in English, therefore, is somewhat hard to interpret, and this difficulty of interpretation seems to relate to the history of these sounds. The splits which produced these developments were the result, it seems, of changes elsewhere in the linguistic system; and these changes were gradual ones.

3.8 In each case several explanations are traditionally offered for these splits. Thus the /f, v/ distinction emerged, it is often held, as a result of the impact of French on the history of English; *vine* and *fine* are loanwords from French, and their appearance in the English lexicon thus affects the phonological structure of the receiving language.

3.9 The distinction between /θ, ð/ arose, probably during the Middle English period, not only as a result of the loss of inflectional endings (giving rise to such near-minimal pairs as *breath : breathe*) but also as a result of lenition in words of low stress, giving rise to pairs such as *thy : thigh.*

3.10 The dating of this latter process has been controversial. It is possible that these lenitions took place as the determiner and pronominal systems evolved in the transition from Old to Middle English. In Old English, the demonstrative system seems to have had an emphatic function which became less significant during the Middle English period, when true definite, along with indefinite, articles emerged (see Stanley 2002: 51–2 for a judicious discussion). Since all such determiners were predictable from context (i.e. at the beginning of a noun phrase), they would naturally be unstressed, and lenis realizations would thus be prototypical. Something similar would happen with pronouns, which were comparatively optional (and thus comparatively emphatic, non-predictable) in Old English, where their present-day 'tracking' discourse functions were carried out to a much greater extent by inflectional endings. In Middle and Modern English, however, pronouns were, like determiners, contextually predictable. This meant that, again, unstressed forms are to be expected, with lenis realizations of the initial consonant.[7]

3.11 Finally, the /s, z/ distinction arose as a result of inflectional loss, as demonstrated by the pair *hūs, hūsian*; the loss of a distinctive infinitive marker *-ian* in the case of the latter gives us the Present-Day English minimal pair *house* (noun) and *house* (verb).

3.12 Two points are worth making here. First, these developments are all 'accidental', relating to developments elsewhere in the system, and they remind us that the history of English sounds cannot be divorced from the history of other parts of the linguistic system. Secondly, no 'new' sound has emerged; as is commonly stated,

---

[7] It is noticeable that Middle and Modern English pronouns, especially in subject/thematic position, are much more formally distinct than they had been in Old English, cf. *he, she, it, they* beside *hē, hēo, hit, hīe*. A functionalist argument would hold that the selection of distinctive variants—*she* in place of *hēo, they* in place of *hīe*—would be favoured in low-stress situations. In such situations, *hēo/hīe* would be hard to distinguish but *she/they,* with distinct initial consonants, could be more easily distinguished even when pronounced with low stress.

'the "accidents" that constitute phonemicisation bring about no more than the realization of... existing potentialities...' (Samuels 1972: 38).

3.13 We can therefore explain split as a phonological phenomenon, but the input to that phonological development derives from phonetic variants which already existed. There were always voiced fricatives; their distribution changed as a result of developments in other levels of language. In short, the voicing of fricatives would seem to be a genuine sound change in that it has a systemic dimension. But this sound change can be explained with reference to changes in other parts of the language, such as grammar and vocabulary. Thus the acceleration of inflectional loss in the Old–Middle English transitional period is traditionally ascribed to contact between English and Norse (see Smith 1996: 154 and references cited there; see also Townend 2002). The influx of French vocabulary, which is a feature distinguishing Middle from Old English, can be related quite directly to English–French cultural relationships after the Norman Conquest of 1066.

3.14 The appearance of the voiced–voiceless distinction in English phonology, therefore, can be explained in historical terms, bringing phonetics and phonology into articulation. Some, however, would find this close connection between phonetics and phonology problematic, and it is to such questions that we should now turn.

4 Why phonology?

4.0 So far in this chapter we have focused on the processes involved in sound change, but some basic ideas about phonetics and phonology have not been examined: this lack should be remedied. Underpinning this book, as has been the case with linguistic enquiry since it began in antiquity, is a concern with classification and the discovery of patterns. Such a concern with patterns in sound brings us into the area of phonology, a subject discussed in the previous chapter but perhaps requiring further unpacking.

4.1 The terminology adopted in this book is that used in the well-established taxonomic-phonemic model whereby *phonemes* and *allophones* are distinguished. To repeat some well-known definitions: the relationship between phoneme and allophone is one of function ('linguistic', 'phonological') to form ('physical', 'phonetic'). Phonemes may be defined either as the smallest speech units that distinguish words from one another in terms of meaning, or as the set of prototypical sounds being aimed at by speakers within a speech community; replacement of one phoneme by another changes the meaning of the word in which it occurs. For example, replacing /b/ with /p/ in *bat* changes the meaning of the word, as it results in *pat*; the pair *bat, pat* is a so-called 'minimal pair'. It is conventional to place phonemes in slash brackets, thus: / ... /. The allophone may be defined as the realization of the phoneme in speech; replacement of one allophone with another realization of the same phoneme does not change the meaning of the word in which it occurs. Replacing [p] with [pʰ] in *pat* does not change the meaning of the word. It is conventional to place allophones in square brackets, thus [...]. Along with 'suprasegmentals' (e.g. stress patterns), phonemes and allophones constitute the level of language known as *accent*. Natural, living, languages have a variety of accents, which vary from person to person, place to place, and social group to social group.

4.2 Phonology, then, can be simply defined: it is to do with the study of sound systems. Some have argued that the phonology–phonetics divide is at the junction between the humanities and the sciences: whereas phonetics can be seen as a branch of physics, phonology is to do with the correlation of sound systems with meanings (see e.g. Giegerich 1992: 31). This distinction is a useful one, even if we may be impatient of the perceived, and perverse, British tendency to emphasize the arts–science divide. Phonology 'makes sense' of the sounds we perceive; it thus brings semantics, which underpins all natural languages, into speech. A grasp of phonology makes it possible for us to relate to human functions the range of sounds we make and hear. As John Wells has indicated with reference to accentual dialectology—though his views have

a wider currency—a refusal to address phonological issues is unsat-
isfactory essentially because '...it is boring. It omits to ask the
questions that linguists find interesting. Not only does it fail to
see the wood for the trees, it declines to acknowledge that trees
can be seen as a wood' (Wells 1982: 41). It would seem, therefore, that
a book on sound change has to address phonological issues from the
outset, and this would seem to articulate with the definition of
sound change arrived at in Chapter 1: *a sound change has taken
place when a variant form, mechanically produced, is imitated by
a second person and that process of imitation causes the system of the
imitating individual to change.* It therefore follows that issues of
system, viz. phonology, have to be at the forefront of discussion.

4.3 But, as even a cursory glance at the scholarly literature will
indicate, phonology is a broad church: there are various phonologies
to choose from, and different scholars have developed different
forms of phonology with very different goals. Indeed, it is commonplace for scholars to be intolerant of models other than their own. In
this chapter, an attempt is made to characterize and contrast different phonological models, and to show how different approaches can
be reconciled and harnessed for the study of sound change.

5 Taxonomic phonology

5.0 As already indicated, the basic terminology adopted in this book
derives from a particular phonological tradition which for some
scholars will seem old-fashioned, namely, taxonomic phonology.

5.1 The operational advantages of traditional taxonomic phonology are fairly clear. It is of course widely recognized and comparatively easily testable: the identification of minimal pairs establishes the
existence of a phoneme. Moreover, it allows for easy comparison of
various phonological systems both diachronically and diatopically
(using the latter term to cover social as well as geographical space).
It can thus be used in combination with what P. A. Luelsdorff has
described as the *Independence Principle*, 'that each dialect may be

adequately described in its own terms, i.e. without reference to the data of related dialects... These independently motivated individual descriptions may then be compared with an eye to pointing out their similarities and differences, leaving the extent and nature of dialect differences an essentially empirical question' (cited Wells 1982: 71–2).

5.2 Such an approach, for instance, underpins A. J. Aitken's study of the Older Scots vowel system:

Basically what I am concerned with doing is reconstructing earlier phonemic systems and specifying as well as the evidence permits the approximate realisations of the phonemes in their different phonetic environments and dialects. Often statements about realisations will be very approximate and are always likely to be much more speculative than statements about the systems. I then show how one system develops into a later one by changes resulting in phonemic mergers and splits and dialectal divergences. Essentially, the outlook and principles are those of a structural dialectologist, concerned with phonemes and their realisations and distributions and with dialectal comparisons of these, except that the comparison is done primarily in the chronological rather than in the regional and social dimension... (2002: xxix)

5.3 Of course, this approach does have certain theoretical limitations. It has been said that 'the aim of the phonology of a language [is] to account for the phonetic regularities that occur in the speech events of that language' (Giegerich 1992: 291). In other words, phonological theory, building on an approach to linguistic enquiry which derives ultimately from the categorizing grammarians of antiquity, is interested in mapping patterns of behaviour which can be generalized across as wide a range of linguistic outputs as possible. The generalizations possible through taxonomic phonology are of course limited, and therefore comparatively weak in comparison with more powerful models, notably various versions of generative phonology.

5.4 Traditional taxonomic phonology is less powerful, and thus perhaps more appropriate as a model if the aim of the enterprise is not to generalize similarities but to distinguish differences. However, such a traditional approach has problems of its own.

5.5 We might take, for example, the phrase *good girl* (cf. Wells 1982: 56). The final -*d* in *good* is, in rapid Present-Day English speech, often realized as [g], and thus the question arises: is [g] in these circumstances an allophone of /d/, since it is environmentally conditioned and no change of meaning results? Yet, as Wells points out, replacement of [g] with [d] in the phrase *big girl* 'would yield the nonsensical **bid girl*. The 'problem' presented by the realization of *-d* in *good girl* arises from a very strict application of taxonomic phonemics, whereby every speech sound has to be assigned to a given phoneme and no other.

5.6 Another problem arises with such pairs as *brewed, brood*. In Scottish accents, such pairs are not homophones, since vowels are realized as long in the environment of morpheme boundaries and a following /r, v, z, d/. This pattern, which seems to have emerged in Scots in the sixteenth century and to have been sustained in Scots and Scottish English ever since, is known as the Scottish Vowel Length Rule, otherwise as 'Aitken's Law' after the scholar who first formulated it precisely (see Aitken 1981; Collinge 1992: 3–6). A strict taxonomic-phonemic approach would posit the existence of phonemic length in Scots, yielding (in this case) /u, uː/. However, it could be argued that such an analysis is uneconomical, and that—given that lengthening is environmentally conditioned—the phenomenon is better seen as allophonic variation. Is the rule, therefore, a sound change? (We will return to this example in 6.6.)

5.7 Such examples demonstrate that taxonomic phonology, if strictly adhered to, presents classificatory difficulties for the student of accentual variation and change.

6 Generative phonology

6.0 Probably the best-established challenge to taxonomic phonology has come from those scholars working in the generative tradition. Of course, generative phonology is itself a very 'broad church', and there are many different models to choose from. However, there are some characteristics that are shared by all generative approaches to language.

6.1 For many years it was common for scholars working with historical materials in the taxonomic tradition to be impatient with generativists of various persuasions working with the same materials, and vice versa; but it is possible that this impatience was based on a mutual misunderstanding of their different but equally valid goals. The generative phonologist is primarily concerned with synchronic description, the reconstruction of the derivational rules and constraints which generate pairs such as *serene–serenity* while allowing pairs such as *even–evenly, nation–nationhood* (but cf. *national*). The purpose of the generative enterprise is, broadly, to map the language faculty, establishing universal phenomena in relation to the rules and/or constraints from which languages and their varieties derive. Explanation, for a generativist, relates to the axiomatic acceptance of the existence of a Language Acquisition Device (see further, most approachably, Pinker 1994; an opposed, equally approachable view, is Sampson 2005).

6.2 Diachronic generative phonology is thus, also in the sense of these terms used in this book, chronological rather than historical, descriptive rather than explanatory in its goals; it is interesting that rules 'account for' rather than 'explain' phenomena, and this distinction is important (see Giegerich 1992: 291, who carefully places 'explain' in inverted commas, or, more straightforwardly, Wells 1982: 69). Although rules based on the analysis of historical materials may be arrayed in chronological order, explanation is not—in the sense of 'explanation' adopted in this book—the aim of generativists: 'rules are not usually presented, or intended, as directly explanatory: they have a language, and indeed dialect-specific role in describing processes, which require explanation externally, perhaps in terms of history, phonetics, memory or acquisition' (McMahon 2000a: 91). It is for this reason that many generativists regularly set aside explanation of linguistic change as uninteresting theoretically or indeed ultimately impossible. We might, for instance, recall Paul Postal's famous characterization of the 'reasons' for language change: 'there is no more reason for languages to change than there is for automobiles to add fins one year and remove them the next, for jackets to have three buttons one year and two the next' (Postal 1968: 283).

In this tradition, the autonomy of linguistics as a discipline is insisted upon; for many working in this tradition, the social factors involved in language change are to be set aside as a distinct scholarly endeavour (see McMahon 1994).

6.3 A descriptive as opposed to explanatory approach is not of course particularly novel. After all, Karl Verner in the second half of the nineteenth century did not set out to *explain* the law that bears his name; he was interested in accounting for the anomalies in Grimm's Law by identifying a *rule which predicted them*, namely,

C [− VOICE] > C [+ VOICE] /_$ [+ STRESS].

6.4 The question is one of fitness for purpose. As Heinz Giegerich puts it, using an attractive parallel:

The 'high-tech' engine of a Porsche will yield greater performance than the 'low-tech' engine of a lawnmower will. But while both produce kinetic energy by means of the internal combustion of petroleum derivatives, it cannot be said that the 'high-tech' version of this device is simply better than the 'low-tech' one. Fitting lawnmowers with Porsche engines would not necessarily improve them. Sports cars and lawnmowers serve different purposes, and the technological devices they contain are suited to those purposes. (Giegerich 1992: 296)

6.5 The *good girl, brewed: brood* problems outlined in Section 5 could be solved in theoretical, descriptive terms by adopting generative approaches. Thus the *good girl* problem could be resolved satisfactorily for generativists by positing the rule /d/ → [g]/_/g/. This rule would relate the phonetic representation to an underlying phonemic representation. Generative phonology takes it as axiomatic that speakers store items as phonemic representations in their mental lexicons; when speakers actually speak, the words and phrases they utter are modified by the application of rules in an ordered way (Wells 1982: 57–8). The rule /d/ → [g]/_/g/ is one such rule.

6.6 The *brewed: brood* problem can be solved similarly though somewhat more subtly, and here the link between synchrony and diachrony comes into play. April McMahon (2000b: *passim*) has argued that Scots, and the prestigious variety of Scottish English known as Scottish Standard English, underwent a sound change in the sixteenth century whereby length was lost as a distinctive feature of vowels; historical 'short' and 'long' vowels were thence distinguished only by quality. However, underlying short vowels were lengthened by rule—the Scottish Vowel Length Rule—in particular environments. This ordering of events would make 'Aitken's Law' a genuine sound change in line with our working definition.

6.7 The difficulty with thorough-going generative phonology for the linguist interested in variation and change is, it has been argued, that it is too powerful. Wells (1982: 59), in his study of the accents of Present-Day English, excludes from consideration phonological–morphological rules which account for pairs such as *serene–serenity* on several grounds, notably because 'they make possible such a large number of rival alleged underlying patterns that disappear into a haze of indeterminacy' (1982: 59). Such a verdict sounds harsh; it could be argued, though, that it is simply a matter of fitness for purpose.

6.8 The version of Generative Phonology known as Lexical Phonology attempts to confront this challenge by trying to keep a close connection between both levels of representation, combating over-abstractness (McMahon 2000b: 6). In Lexical Phonology, systems emerge from the interaction of variants, involving 'lexeme-by-lexeme phonemic redistribution' (McMahon 2000b: 214). Lexical Phonology thus allows for the incorporation of variation into generative theory, something not commonly discussed by generativists hitherto: '[Lexical Phonology] encourages a view whereby even different speakers may have different underlying representations and rule systems . . . This in turn allows potential incorporation of insights from sociolinguistics . . . , where cumulative innovations by individual speakers are recognised as the key to understanding language variation and change' (McMahon 2000b: 212). It will be clear from this description that Lexical Phonology is a model congruent with the themes of this book, as outlined in Chapter 1. (For a brief conspectus of Lexical Phonology in the wider context of generative linguistics, see Giegerich 1992: 313. See McMahon 2000b for a thorough-going application of Lexical Phonology to the history of English; for an introductory account, see McMahon 1994: 64–8.)

6.9 However, it is interesting that McMahon sees Lexical Phonology as incorporating 'insights' from sociolinguistics; sociolinguistic enquiry is seen as a distinct endeavour, contributing to the theory, rather than vice versa. Such a formulation would seem to support the view that generative linguists are interested in description, not explanation in the sense adopted in this book.

6.10 We might therefore turn the argument round: what can generative phonology offer explanatory diachronic linguistics? I would argue that generative phonology (in its Lexical Phonology guise) offers scholars interested in explanation a more precise definition of what is meant by a sound change. The key insight to be adopted from most versions of generative linguistics is to do with the notion of the 'rule'. The term *rule*—like *law* as established by an earlier generation of linguists—is in some ways unfortunate. The term is derived from the formal study of mathematics or philosophy and arguably too hedged about for non-linguists with connotations of prescription for the study of dynamic, protean phenomena such as human language. But the notion which underlies the term is valuable: to refer to rules emphasizes that it is possible to describe a particular linguistic phenomenon in an ordered way. More particularly, the term emphasizes explicitly that there is an abstraction that underpins the classification of individual sounds—namely, the underlying representation already referred to.[8]

6.11 The notion of the abstract underlying representation, of course, is not unique to generative linguistics; indeed, it underpins the whole definition of the phoneme ever since the notion was first distinguished. The idea of the phoneme as a unitary mental entity goes back at least to the early twentieth-century linguist Edward Sapir (cf. Taylor 1996: 228). In this sense, generative phonology,

---

[8] More radical generative approaches include Optimality Theory, which has sometimes been presented as explanatory in the terms of this book. For a comprehensive critique of the theory's descriptive and explanatory adequacy, see McMahon (2000a: 92–100); the arguments presented in this publication are too complex for swift rehearsal, but for our purposes it suffices to say that the theory does not seek to explain forms in the sense adopted in this book. For that reason, Optimality Theory is not discussed further here.

despite the frequent claims of novelty made by many of its practitioners, remains within a clear tradition of linguistic enquiry.

6.12 Let us conclude this section by examining once again the phrase *good girl*. Is the realization [g] in this environment a sound change? The answer must be 'no', given that there is no change in the underlying representation: realizations in [g] are solely found in a particular environment and are not generalized from there. (Something similar happens with the realization of /nd/ in *handbag*, where, in relaxed-style pronunciation, [m] is common.) If the realization [g] became much more general rather than conditioned by its special environment then we could start to argue that a sound change, /d/ > /g/, had taken place; that does not happen here, since no such realization occurs in (e.g.) *good boy, good woman, good friend*, etc., where different developments can take place (e.g. the final plosive in *good* being realized as [b] in *good boy*).

6.13 It would seem, therefore, that generalization of a variant is the key to distinguishing sound change from simple allophonic variation. Scholars such as William S.-Y. Wang and Mieko Ogura have shown that this generalization seems to take place from environment to environment and word to word, as part of 'lexical diffusion' (see e.g. Wang 1969; Ogura 1987, 1990). Such diffusion may be seen as the gradual operation of analogical processes. And Lexical Phonology, which suggests that underlying representations vary from speaker to speaker, fits rather well with the contact-based approach to language change which was described in Chapter 1 (see McMahon 2000b: 214 and references there).

6.14 Lexical Phonology, therefore, helps us develop a more precise understanding of what we mean by the term 'system' in our definition of sound change: *a sound change has taken place when a variant form, mechanically produced, is imitated by a second person and that process of imitation causes the system of the imitating individual to change*. In Lexical Phonology, as was stated in 6.8, systems emerge from the interaction of variants. It is to this process of emergence that we will now turn, and in doing so, further phonological models will be discussed, namely Natural and Evolutionary Phonology.

7 Natural and Evolutionary Phonology

7.0 An approach in terms of gradience underpins several other recent approaches to phonology such as Natural Phonology (see Donegan and Stampe 1979) and Dependency Phonology (see Anderson and Ewen 1987), and it is therefore not surprising that the latter, in particular, has found favour with scholars interested in modelling historical changes (e.g. Jones 1989). Some such modellings retain the asocial stance of early generativism, and for that reason are not adopted here; but others are socially informed. Thus the theoretical model underlying Natural Phonology has been described in the following terms: '...language is not a passive unfolding of pre-wired competence but a creative confrontation, within, of course, the limits imposed by human biology, between the speaker and his language, a historically derived and socially encrusted institution' (Singh, in Hurch and Rhodes 1996: 4). Like Lexical Phonology, such an approach would seem to be congruent with that adopted in this book.

7.1 Natural Phonology developed its own conventions and notations, but its basic tenets are clearly related to some older ideas, notably functionalist ones of the kind discussed earlier in this chapter:

Natural phonology['s]...basic thesis is that the living sound patterns of languages, in their development in each individual as well as their evolution over the centuries, are governed by forces implicit in human vocalization and perception. (Donegan and Stampe 1979: 126)

Classical Natural Phonology divides segmental processes into two types, fortitions and lenitions. Whereas the former arise from acoustic and perceptual considerations and thus contribute to making speech more easily perceptible, the latter allow for ease of articulation. The function of processes is to adapt language to the needs of both speakers and hearers. A process simply ameliorates an articulatory difficulty present in its input structure or rectifies a perceptual difficulty, be it segmental, sequential, or prosodic. (Hurch and Rhodes 1996: x)

7.2 It will be observed from these quotations that Natural Phonology does not draw a clear line between phonological and phonetic enquiry; the connection, and not the distinction, between phonology and phonetics is insisted upon. This connection between phonology and phonetics is also part of a more recent model, Evolutionary Phonology. Evolutionary Phonology, furthermore, goes beyond Natural Phonology in attempting to break down the perceived barrier between synchronic and diachronic linguistics. The theory is concerned, in Juliette Blevins's words, to demonstrate 'that a broad range of phonological phenomena can be explained in terms of common phonetically motivated sound change' (2004: 7). It draws on two 'uncontroversial' (Blevins's term) observations:

1. 'all spoken language is characterized by a wide range of phonetic variation, some of which is language specific, and some of which is determined by the physical properties of the human vocal apparatus.' (Blevins 2004: 7–8)
2. 'though language transmission from one generation to the next is constrained by perceptual, articulatory, cognitive, and social factors, language transmission is, by its very nature, indirect and imperfect.' (Blevins 2004: 8)

7.3 It will be clear from this characterisation that Evolutionary Phonology fits rather well with the 'H&H' model discussed in Chapter 1, and this connection is explicitly made by Blevins in her comprehensive discussion.[9]

7.4 A key component of Evolutionary Phonology as developed by Blevins is that it is in her terms non-functionalist (or, more properly, 'largely non-functionalist', 2004: 16). Blevins argues that sound change is inherently non-optimizing—surely *any* change must introduce communicative barriers?—and therefore non-teleological: 'Sound change happens because of the way in which we produce and hear speech. It does not happen in order to improve speech in any way' (Blevins 2004: 16). Such an argument seems unexceptional.

---

[9] Blevins (2004: 36–7, n. 20) does draw a careful distinction between Evolutionary Phonology and 'H&H' approaches: 'Evolutionary Phonology adopts the H&H *description* of intraspeaker variation as a function of the hyper- to hypoarticulated speech continuum. However, unlike H&H theory, it does not view sound change as "improving" speech along this continuum. Rather, a stochastic model is adopted in which changes in frequency of particular phonetic variants result in shifts along the hyper- to hypoarticulation axis.'

But the point Blevins goes on to make is that—and this is where the evolutionary metaphor is so useful—sound change exists as part of the struggle to express meaning comparable with the Darwinian 'struggle for life'. Semantics underpins all language; we are in error if we decide to explore one part of language (phonology, grammar, lexicon) without reference to other parts. In this evolutionary framework, and using Blevins's terminology, a mutation arises through CHANCE, but the CHOICE of a variant is favoured because of the environment—the dynamically changing environment—within which the variant fleetingly exists.

7.5 Blevins's work is exciting not only because it brings synchronic and diachronic linguistics into articulation but also because it brings phonetics and phonology back together. However, Blevins limits her discussion as follows: '...all sound changes explored in this book are examined at the level of the individual language learner' (Blevins 2004: 19). Although this approach would seem to connect with the approach discussed in the previous chapter—that change can be distinguished at the level of the individual—there is a difference. Blevins's approach is a valuable simplification for the purposes of her argument, but it means that she misses the social working of speech, which seems to be a crucial factor in its development. Language is a shared tool. And like all shared tools it is shaped differently by different users within a framework of monitoring. As Samuels puts it, '...the production of new variants is mainly articulatory in nature, their spread and imitation mainly acoustic, and both are continually coordinated by the process of monitoring.' (1972: 31)

7.6 This last statement would seem to fit well with our working definition of sound change: *a sound change has taken place when a variant form, mechanically produced, is imitated by a second person and that process of imitation causes the system of the imitating individual to change.*

7.7 In other words, forms and functions go together, and both have to be borne in mind in a discussion of the evolution of sounds. It could be argued therefore that, by making her approach non-functionalist in a broad sense—therapeutic but non-teleological—Blevins is missing a key component of linguistic enquiry, namely, its social functioning. This component is insisted upon in the current book.

8 A theoretical framework

8.0 It will have been observed that the various approaches outlined above—and it should be emphasized that the constraints of space make these outlines very crude and un-nuanced—all have virtues. Bearing this in mind, the approach of this book is eclectic. It uses the terminology of taxonomic phonology, which has advantages of simplicity and being widely understood, but notes the usefulness of the notion of the abstract underlying representation as presented in the generative model known as Lexical Phonology. Its theoretical orientation may also be related to recent insights developed within Evolutionary Phonology. But it also notes that explanation for sound change has to be located in social change, and that the old distinction between 'internal' and 'external' linguistic history has to be broken down (for an interesting discussion of the slippery nature of these terms, see McMahon 2000b: 1–5). Taken together, this approach may be described as cognitive.

8.1 Cognitive linguistics has been defined thus:

Whereas generativists regard knowledge of language as an autonomous component of the mind, independent, in principle, from other kinds of knowledge and from other cognitive skills, cognitivists posit an intimate, dialectic relationship between the structure and function of language on the one hand, and non-linguistic skills and knowledge on the other.   (Taylor 1996: ix)

It will be clear from what follows that this theoretical stance underpins much of the argument of this book. Intralinguistic development is seen as intimately related to extralinguistic development: language, an inherently social phenomenon, is thus linked to socio-historical development, and its history should be seen within the framework of human history. Language change therefore reflects 'the lives, purposes and aspirations of the human beings that language serves' (Samuels 1972: 181): explanations for language change are to be found in the social functioning of language. This insight can be used to explain language change in general, and sound change in particular. This chapter will conclude with an extended demonstration of how such an explanation is possible, even for a development which is comparatively remote historically.

9 An extended example: Grimm's Law

9.0 This chapter concludes with a discussion of a sound change which brings together the theoretical insights developed so far, namely, Grimm's Law, otherwise known as the First Consonant Shift. This Shift is perhaps the best known of all sound changes (see Collinge 1992: 63–76); but Grimm's discussion is a description, not an explanation (see Chapter 1, 1.8, and also 1.4, above). Is it possible to *explain* Grimm's Law historically?

9.1 The First Consonant Shift is a chain shift, that is to say that change in one part of the system is followed by change elsewhere. The traditional approach to chain shifts is to refer to 'drag chains', where a neighbouring sound is 'dragged' into a phonological slot vacated by another sound, and 'push chains', whereby a neighbouring sound is forced to vacate a slot because of encroachments on that slot by another sound. The notions are illustrated diagrammatically in Figure 3.2.

9.2 However, such an account of a sound shift is, it may be argued, rather abstract, and it is worth unpacking the processes involved. Underpinning the process seems to be the notion of *phonological space*. An individual phoneme occupies a fairly broad

Drag chain: 1. Sound A vacates phonological space
2. Sound B occupies space vacated by Sound A

Push chain: 1. Sound B impinges on phonological space occupied by Sound A
2. Sound A moves away from Sound B

B ⟶ A ⟶

FIGURE 3.2 Drag and push chains

slot in the langue within which it is situated, and its phonetic realizations (within parole) can therefore vary very widely in terms of pitch, amplitude, and timbre while still being considered a 'single' sound in contrastive terms. It is likely that, in a given speech community, there will be a prototypical realization, but that prototypical realization will simply be at the centre of a range of quite different realizations. (For a schematic representation of phonological space, see Figure 1.2).

9.3 How 'real' this phenomenon is can be established through observation of sound patterns which actually exist. Figure 3.3 (after Lieberman 1984: ch. 7) is an attempt to demonstrate what a phonological space actually looks like in terms of measured realizations, through plotting on a graph the recorded sound frequencies (in Hz = Hertz) at two points in the production of resonances, that is, the notes made by the vibration of air, within the vocal tract: at the

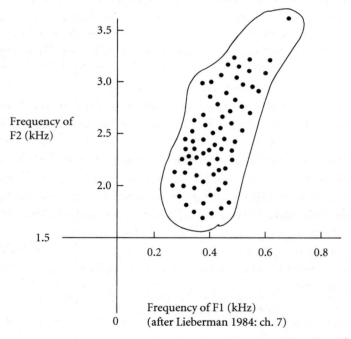

FIGURE 3.3 Realizations of the vowel phoneme /ɪ/ produced by seventy-six different speakers in terms of recorded sound frequencies

back of the vocal tract (first formant $= F_1$) and in the front of the mouth (second formant $= F_2$) (for details, see Ladefoged 2001: 33–4).

9.4 Such variation arises through the competing forces of two major principles, long recognized by linguists. A good summary is offered by Paul Boersma (1998: 107), who cites nineteenth-century authorities such as Paul Passy and Henry Sweet:

1) Languages tend to get rid of anything superfluous. This principle could be called the *law of least effort*, but Passy prefers (after Sweet) the term *principle of economy*, as it is also assumed to trigger processes like the loss of unaccented vowels, which presumably trades the articulatory effort of the resulting consonant clusters for the smaller time needed to finish the utterance. Among the processes ascribed to this principle are the weakening of accent and the subsequent loss or paradigmatic merger of sounds in unimportant syllables, the simplification of consonant clusters, assimilation, and the abridgement of long vowels.

2) Languages tend to stress or exaggerate anything that is necessary. This is the *principle of emphasis*. First, processes like aspiration and affrication of plosives are considered to be due to this principle, as well as vowel epenthesis, glide insertion, dissimilation, and the change of approximants into fricatives or plosives. The second action of this principle is that of increasing the distinction between two sounds in order to reduce confusion between different words.

9.5 The competition between these forces produces variation within phonological space. Such variation is not inefficient, but communicatively necessary. Any two speakers will have, to a greater or lesser extent, as the result of slight physiological and social differences, and also depending on the style being adopted ('forceful', 'relaxed'), a differing set of realizations for a particular phoneme, and it is therefore important for communicative purposes for each speaker to have a fairly wide tolerance of others' usages.

9.6 In such circumstances, it is easy to conceive not only of a situation where overlap between systems might occur, but also the results of such an overlap. Such a situation is illustrated schematically in Figure 3.4. Community A has a phonological space with a prototypical realization alpha; Community B has an overlapping phonological space with a prototypical realization beta. The two phonemes are used in the same lexical items in each community.

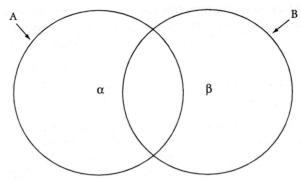

Phoneme /X/ is realized by Community A within phonological space A, with prototypical realization α 'alpha'. Phoneme /X/ is realized by Community B within phonological space B, with prototypical realization β 'beta'

FIGURE 3.4 Overlap of phonological spaces

If Community A comes into contact with Community B, and Community A wishes to respond to the social dominance of Community B expressed in speech, then speakers within Community A will begin to favour realizations closer to Community B's prototypical usage within the items in question. And if Community B's prototypical usage is outside the phonological space with which Community A started, then 'missing the target' or (to put it in more up-to-date terms) hyper-/hypoadaptations can be expected to occur (see Stuart-Smith 2004: *passim*, and references there). Such adaptations parallel the imperfect replications characteristic of evolutionary systems.

9.7 Processes such as these underpin the kinds of recorded readjustment which are often cited in the scholarly literature, which entail the reorganization of phonological space consequent on the appearance of new phonemes see, for example, Moulton 1962. Moulton's findings have been crisply summarised by Samuels: 'Swiss dialects possessing the three phonemes /ɑː/, /æː/ and /ɔː/ use only central allophones of /ɑː/, whereas those with only the two phonemes /ɑː/ and /æː/ have a greater allophonic range for /ɑː/ and typically show a more retracted vowel' (1972: 31). Samuels gives a very clear outline of the process involved:

Each phoneme, ideally, must remain at a point of full, if not always maximum, differentiation from its neighbours in its system (vocalic or consonantal), so that the groups of words in which it occurs remain distinguished and viable. If one phoneme shifts, others will also shift in such a way that the differentiation is preserved ('push-chain mechanism'), while others again will automatically increase their area of possible realization by moving into the vacated space ('drag-chain mechanism'). (1972: 31)

9.8 This process can be couched in less abstract terms. Speakers constantly adjust their pronunciations as part of linguistic monitoring to take account of feedback from interlocutors. If the feedback is unfavourable (e.g. incomprehension, stigmatisation), then other variants will be adopted which avoid such unfavourable feedback. Such situations will be especially encouraged in situations of social disturbance. Underpinning the whole process is the semantic level: the struggle to sustain various kinds of meaning (see Anttila 1989: 77; *pace* Lass 1997: ch. 7).

9.9 Chain shifts, then, can be seen as a reaction to such processes, since phonological spaces, fairly obviously, must be seen not simply as a collection of realizations but also contrastively. Hyper- and hypoadaptations mean the adoption of features not within the original phonological space but within *neighbouring* phonological spaces. And such developments will have a knock-on effect elsewhere in the system; in other words, a chain shift will have taken place.

9.10 The First Consonant Shift can, in terms of phonetics and phonology, be fairly convincingly fitted into such a development. To illustrate the point, one component of the Shift will be explored, the development which results in such pairs as Latin *frater*–English *brother*, Greek *kannabis*–English *hemp* (< Old English *hænep*), Latin *piscis*–English *fish*.

9.11 We might take the last example first. It is worth observing that, in the Present-Day descendants of Latin (e.g. Italian, French, Spanish), /p/ differs in its prototypical realization from /p/ in the Germanic languages (e.g. German, Dutch, English). In Germanic languages, prototypical realizations of /p/ are aspirated (there is a short delay after the closure is released, allowing the air to rush out) before the following vowel. Such aspiration is particularly noticeable when /p/ occurs in stressed syllables (see Ladefoged 2001: 120; Gimson 1989: 151 ff.).

9.12 It is an observable fact that aspirated /p/ can be realized in Present-Day English in what is known as an affricated form: 'If the release of plosive closures is not made rapidly, a fricative sound, articulated in the same area of articulation as the plosive, will be heard; plosives made with this slow, fricative release are said to be *affricated*' (Gimson 1989: 160). Such realizations are obviously very near to the prototypical realizations for /f/ in Present-Day English. The phonological change /p/ > /f/, therefore, can be seen as phonetically plausible, as a hyperadaptation based upon aspirated realizations of /p/.

9.13 The contrast /b/–/p/ may be studied next. Here, too, phonetic processes observable in Present-Day English, to do with 'lenis' and 'fortis' realizations, are helpful: 'Those English consonants which are usually voiced tend to be articulated with relatively weak energy [i.e. lenis], whereas those which are voiceless are relatively strong [i.e. fortis]' (Gimson 1989: 34). However, as Gimson points out, lenis articulations of /p/, which can easily be reproduced as [b], are quite common—another overlap in phonological space.

9.14 Finally, we might examine the /f/–/b/ contrast. It is observable that many foreign speakers of English, notably Germans, have a habit of using a bilabial fricative [ß] in place of English [f] (Gimson 1989: 183). Now [ß] is also found in English as an affricated realization of /b/ (Gimson 1989: 160); such realizations suggests that there is the potential for overlap in phonological space.

9.15 In short, in all three sounds which were affected by Grimm's Law—/b/, /p/, /f/—there is evidence from Present-Day English of allophonic variation which would allow for the Shift to develop within the phonological spaces occupied by the affected consonants. Such evidence from present-day behaviour, given that the vocal tracts of humans in the past are much the same as those of the present, can be adduced as part of the story. In other words, it is important, when dealing with materials from the extreme past, to operate within the bounds of 'phonetic plausibility'; hypotheses can be evaluated in these terms (for 'the evaluative criterion of phonetic plausibility', see Stuart-Smith 2004: 159).[10]

9.16 That the First Consonant Shift represents a series of plausible sound changes, given the evidence of (*inter alia*) Present-Day English, would seem, therefore, established. But it is important to grasp that simply establishing that variants can exist does not mean that 'sound change' is thus in any way *explained* in historical terms. As was pointed out in Chapter 1, it is quite possible for a congeries of variant realizations to exist for a particular phoneme without a 'sound change' actually happening: to repeat Roger Lass's statement, 'stable variation is one of the common states of language' (1997: 304). The questions remain: why then? Why there? Together these questions make up the 'actuation problem' for Grimm's Law.

10 Explaining Grimm's Law (I): phonetic processes

10.0 Before addressing the actuation problem directly, it is worth noting that there is a parallel to the Shift elsewhere within the Indo-European group of families. As was pointed out by Antoine Meillet many years ago, a comparable shift also occurs in Armenian, a variety of Indo-European which is otherwise formally very different from Germanic and geographically very distant.

10.1 Two explanations may be offered to deal with this similarity. On the one hand, Germanic and Armenian—both of which are, as it happens, on the periphery of the primary geographical extent of the Indo-European group of languages, albeit at opposite ends—may retain archaic features lost in the more central varieties. There are parallels for such a pattern; cultural phenomena tend to be at their most archaic on a culture's periphery. The alternative explanation, however, not quite so unlikely as it might seem, is that the same outcome can arise for different reasons.

---

[10] The shift from aspirated plosive to fricative is well known in the history of other languages. For instance, in the history of Greek, the aspirated plosives *phi*, *theta*, and *chi* all developed into fricatives (Allen 1978: 27).

10.2 The triggering of the Armenian Consonant Shift has generally been held to be a contact-induced phenomenon, the result of
interaction with neighbouring languages in the Caucasus moun-
tains: 'It remains striking, however, that the Armenian system of
stops [i.e. plosives] and affricates, with its triple series of voiceless,
voiceless aspirated, and voiced sounds, is the same as that of the
Georgian' (Meillet 1967: 122; but see also Stuart-Smith 2004: 191–3
and references there cited for a more nuanced discussion).

10.3 Is it possible to argue for a similar, contact-induced triggering of the Germanic Consonant Shift? Meillet (and others) assumed
so, but confessed that the 'influence...remains enigmatic' (Meillet
1967: 123). An attempt to link the Germanic Shift to contact with
Celtic (cf. Meillet 1967: 122–3 and references therein) was unsuccess-
ful, not least because Celtic has, unlike Georgian, no comparable
consonant inventory.

10.4 However, Helmut Esau's discussion (1973) of the triggering
of the Germanic Shift has suggested a more plausible source: contact
between the Germanic peoples and the tribes they encountered
during their southward movement in the first few centuries BC—a
period of major change in Germanic society, as historians have long
acknowledged (see Thompson 1965: 2). As the Germanic peoples
moved south they encountered a group of people known to the
Romans as *Raeti*, first mentioned by Polybius, a Greek historian
working in Rome in the second century BC. The Raeti seem to have
been a mixed Celtic–Illyrian people whose language contained certain 'pre-Italic' elements related to Etruscan (see Whatmough 1937).
They lived in the Alpine passes in the borderlands between modern
Austria, Switzerland, and Italy, and were ultimately incorporated
into the Roman Empire towards the end of the first century BC.

10.5 The encounter with the Raeti seems to correspond in date
with the Shift, and Esau suggests that the Shift is related to this
encounter. To grasp his argument, further engagement with some
quite precise phonetic detail is necessary.

10.6 Raetic seems to have had two series of obstruents: /p, t, k/
and /f, θ, k/. (For a definition of the term *obstruent*, see Giegerich
1992: 20, who describes this manner of articulation as one which

'involves an obstruction of the air stream that produces a phonetic effect independent of voicing'. See also Chapter 5, 3.5.) These two series were primarily distinguished by the plosive–fricative distinction; both series were voiceless. A secondary distinction seems to have been aspiration; /f, θ, k/ were pronounced with aspiration, /p, t, k/ without. However, aspiration was not, in Raetic, of crucial importance; voice, being more salient acoustically, was the primary distinctive feature.

10.7 The pre-Germanic system of obstruents—that is, the system which existed before the operation of Grimm's Law—had an extra contrast alongside voice and aspiration (see Esau 1973: 468). This extra contrast depended on the feature known as *murmur* or *whispery voice*, which is used phonemically in, for example, Hindi (for details see Catford 1988: 55).

10.8 Acoustically, murmur and aspiration are very similar, and in a situation of language contact it seems likely that aspiration, a secondary or 'redundant' feature in both systems before they came into contact, became a primary contrast during a process of hyper-/hypo-adaptation. The output would be a reinterpreted system, where the phonemic contrasts between /p, t, k/, /b, d, g/, and /bh, dh, gh/ in pre-Germanic would be based on two features: voice and aspiration (see Esau 1973: 469).

10.9 The next step in the development seems fairly clear. Aspiration went with fricative sounds in Raetic, and, in a situation of continuing, dynamic hyper-/hypo-adaptation, fricativity replaced aspiration as a primary contrast. In Pre-Germanic, /p, t, k/ had aspiration; replacement of aspiration with fricativity as a Germanic response to contact with Raetic would result in /f, θ, x/. The only non-aspirated non-fricative obstruents in the reinterpreted Pre-Germanic system were /b, d, g/; in Raetic, the only non-aspirated and non-fricative obstruents were /p, t, k/. A reinterpretation of /b, d, g/ as voiceless /p, t, k/ would therefore be another adaptive strategy as Germanic speakers encountered Raetic usage; the development would be possible once Pre-Germanic /p, t, k/ had changed to /f, θ, x /, thus vacating the necessary phonological space. /bh, dh, gh/, voiced aspirated plosives, were reinterpreted in Germanic as voiced fricatives /ß, ð, γ/ as aspiration was replaced by fricative-ness as a distinctive feature of obstruents; a later shift to /b, d, g/ would be possible once Pre-Germanic /b, d, g/ had undergone their own shift to /p, t, k/. Such outputs would represent the triggering of the First Consonant Shift. The development is a very small step; but in language, as in other dynamically complex systems, very small developments can have big effects.

10.10 Confirmation of the importance of 'phonetic insight' in understanding these developments is offered by some exceptions to the process. /p, t, k/ do not undergo the Shift when they are the second element of a voiceless consonant cluster, and this failure can be accounted for if the previous discussion is accepted. It is observable in Present-Day English that aspiration of /p, t, k/ fails when preceded by an alveolar fricative; this lack of aspiration would mean that fricativity would not develop in its place, and thus /p, t, k/ would be retained.

10.11 In sum, the First Consonant Shift may be seen as a development whereby, in a situation of language contact, various hyper-/hypoadaptive strategies were adopted; alternative articulations were exploited to sustain distinctiveness within the constraints of phonological space. The Shift can thus be fitted rather well into the framework suggested in Chapter 1. Incoming groups, with weak social ties of the kind to be expected during a period of immigration and mixing, made minor adjustments of pronunciation in conditions where hyper-/hypo-adaptation was likely to be favoured.

11 Explaining Grimm's Law (II): extralinguistic correspondences

11.0 Esau's interpretation articulates with the extralinguistic evidence, slight though it may be, and it is at this point that we should look briefly at the evidence for the dating of the Shift.

11.1 The dating of the First Consonant Shift is a traditional problem for linguistic historians. Two pieces of external evidence are usually adduced, one supplied by the Greek historian Herodotus, who seems to have died *c.*420 BC, and another by an inscription on the Negau helmet, which is usually dated to the third century BC. Herodotus refers to *kannabis* as a substance recently introduced to the Greeks by people he calls Scythians; *kannabis* is thus a loanword into Greek from the language of the Scythians. *Kannabis* is cognate with the Germanic word *hemp* (Old English *haenep*), and a comparison of these cognates would seem to display two components of the Shift: $k > h$, $b > p$. At first sight, it would seem that the Shift had not taken place by the time of Herodotus.

11.2 However, an immediate qualification is necessary. The term *Scythian* is a loose one; according to the Greek navigator Pytheas, who travelled extensively around the coasts of northern Europe in the fourth century BC, the Scythians occupied lands which extended from the Carpathians to the shores of the North Sea, and included tribes such as the Gutones and Teutones, usually identified with the Germans. A distinctive Germanic group is first—possibly—distinguished only in the first century BC, in the writings of the Syrian philosopher Posidonios, whose *Histories* survive in fragmentary form. The argument that the Scythians who referred to *kannabis* were speaking in a language which subsequently developed into Proto-Germanic thus remains heavily qualified.

11.3 The second piece of evidence is similarly problematic. In 1812, at Negau on the border between Austria and the former republic of Yugoslavia, in modern Slovenia, a set of bronze helmets was discovered. On one of these, in North Italic letters, was the inscription which may be transliterated as *hariXasti teiva*, usually interpreted as meaning 'to the god Herigast' (Elliott 1959: 9; for an illustration, see Elliott 1959: Plate I). The form *teiva*, it could be argued, is cognate with Latin *divus* 'godlike'—compare *deus* 'god'—and would thus indicate a sound shift $d > t$, a development which is part of the Consonant Shift. Most scholars date the Negau helmets to the third or second centuries BC, and thus the Shift can be seen as having taken place by that time.

11.4 However, there are major problems with seeing the Negau helmet as conclusive evidence for such a development. The dating

and the interpretation of the inscription have both proved controversial; indeed, Robert Nedoma (1995: 45) has argued that *teiva* is
a second name in apposition with *hariXasti*, though it may be a
copying of, or a parallel to, the Roman habit of linking divinity with
their leaders, for example 'the divine Augustus', on the model of the
heroic epithet—compare *pius Aeneas*. Moreover, there is evidence
that Germanic peoples tended not to wear metal helmets, preferring
lighter leather caps in order to sustain their mobility, their chief
advantage in battle. However, the Germanic habit of acting as
mercenaries for others—first for the Celts, later for the Romans—
make it probable that some adopted from the Celts the habit of
wearing metal helmets, as recorded by Diodorus Siculus, whose
historical compilation dates from the end of the first century BC,
and there is later evidence that individuals who were prominent in
Germanic society, at any rate, adopted helmets as a sign of their
status (see further Wilson 1981: 128).

11.5 Perhaps more convincing is the evidence of names. Esau
notes that Latin names for Germanic tribes demonstrate both
shifted and unshifted forms: thus the names Cimbri and Teutoni
are unshifted, whereas such names as Chatti and Cheruski are
shifted, the <ch> spelling characteristically being used in Latin to
represent an aspirated plosive, distinct from <c> to be found
prototypically, though not exclusively, in loanwords (Allen 1978:
26–7; cf. the present-day German place name *Hessen*). 'If we examine the unshifted forms, we notice that these are the names of tribes
with which the Romans came into contact first, approximately
during the second century BC. The shifted forms, on the other
hand, represent the names of tribes which the Romans encountered
somewhat later' (Esau 1973: 465). This contrast would suggest that
the shift took place after the time when the Romans encountered the
Cimbri, but before the time when they encountered the Chatti; the
priority of the Cimbri and Teutoni is indicated by the habitual
reference by Roman writers to *terror Cimbricus* and *furor Teutonicus*
when describing Germanic belligerence. Such an interpretation
is supported by the historical record: the Cimbri, for instance,
are first described as defeating a Roman consular army at Noricum

in 113 BC, while the Chatti were the most powerful enemy of the Romans in the following century, in persistent warfare with the early Roman emperors as well as with neighbouring Germanic tribes.

11.6 Despite these indications, however, it has to be admitted that the direct evidence for the dating of the Shift is very uncertain. Nevertheless, there is even less evidence for earlier datings, and for this early period it is important to use all the indications to hand. As Esau has stated, 'At best we can say that 500–100 BC appears as attractive as any other explanation offered so far' (Esau 1973: 457). For the time being, therefore, this date will be accepted here.

11.7 If the dating is accepted, then there is, it might be argued, a working hypothesis at least for the actuation of the First Consonant Shift. Noricum, where the Cimbri defeated the Romans, is on the Raetian border, and Esau has argued that the encounter between Germanic tribes and the Raeti was the extralinguistic trigger for the Shift. Grimm's Law can therefore be explained, with at least a degree of plausibility, as the result of a socially situated 'H&H' process at a particular point in time.

11.8 It must, of course, be admitted that this explanation for Grimm's Law, although possibly the best available, is extremely tentative given the limitations of the evidence, even if plausible in theoretical terms. In the following three chapters, some case studies in the history of English will be investigated, and explanations of increasing plausibility, using the evidence which comes down to us from three distinct periods, will be explored.

4

From Pre-English to Old English

1 'Pre-English'

1.0 As was discussed in Chapter 2, the 'tree' and 'wave' models of linguistic relationships are extremely useful for linguists. However, it has already been emphasized that there are limitations to such models, which are essentially post-hoc formulations not really capturing the processual and dynamic character of language change.

1.1 The relationship of English to the other Germanic languages is not an exception to this rule. In a simple tree model such as Figure 4.1, for instance, English is a daughter language along with the others of the West Germanic group: German, Dutch, and Afrikaans, all of which are seen as deriving from a common ancestor, Proto-West Germanic, which itself derives from Proto-Germanic, which itself derives from the so-called 'centum' node of Indo-European languages. Such models are commonplace in textbooks on historical linguistics.

1.2 But, as was indicated in Chapter 2, such models need clarifying. The lines which connect the various nodes summarize periods of considerable complexity; such complexity is to be expected, given the limitations of tree models (see Chapter 2, in particular Section 5). Thus the lines which connect the various nodes represent periods of divergence between different languages, the so-called 'pre-' languages. It was during one of these processes of divergence, the 'pre-Germanic' period, that the sound change known as Grimm's Law took place. Similarly, we can refer to the 'pre-English' period of

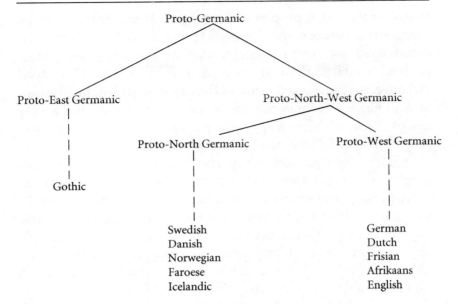

FIGURE 4.1 The Germanic family of languages

divergence which resulted in the appearance of what may reasonably be considered a discrete language. However, even this categorization may be too simple; as we shall see in this chapter, the earliest form of English, Old English, is itself a portmanteau term for a set of varieties which have distinct origins.

1.3 The speakers of what were to become the Germanic languages seem to have originated, possibly in the fifth and fourth centuries BC, in what has been referred to as 'that bottleneck of the Baltic which is constituted by present-day Denmark and southern Sweden' (Haugen 1976: 100). In the sixth century AD, the writer Jordanes, probably himself of Germanic origin though writing in Latin, referred to Scandinavia as *vagina gentium*, 'a womb of peoples', and this description—if extended to the north of Germany between the rivers Weser and Oder—seems to be an accurate one, even though it should be recognized that Jordanes was referring to events which took place perhaps a thousand years before he was born.

1.4 From this area of origin the Germanic peoples spread south and east; their spread to the west was constrained by resistance from first the Celtic peoples and subsequently the Roman empire. Antagonism between the Germanic peoples and the others they encountered was not consistent, warfare alternating with more peaceful contacts through trade and other forms of cultural exchange. And towards the end of the imperial period, the Romans took to hiring large numbers of Germanic mercenaries as auxiliary troops (*foederati, laeti*); many of the great generals of the late Roman period, such as Stilicho, were of Germanic origin.

1.5 The language spoken by the first identifiable Germanic peoples was Proto-Germanic, which is the presumed common ancestor of all the modern Germanic languages. Proto-Germanic, like all natural languages, cannot have been homogeneous, and it is likely that the differences between its dialects—which subsequently developed into distinct languages—were present from the outset. This proto-variety itself eventually split into three further groups, commonly referred to as East, North, and West Germanic. Most modern scholars are of the opinion that an initial split led to the emergence of two proto-languages, Proto-East Germanic on the one hand, and Proto-North-West Germanic on the other. Subsequently, it is held that two further proto-languages emerged from the latter: Proto-North Germanic and Proto-West Germanic.

1.6 This picture is schematic, and almost certainly a gross oversimplification, for reasons already given at the beginning of this chapter. The evidence indicates that at least the West and North Germanic groups, because of geographical proximity, continued to interact, resulting in a series of contact-induced developments; it has been said that the Germanic varieties 'do not strive to part from one another, but remain in ever-changing connection with one another' (Rösel 1962: 120, cited in and translated by Haugen 1976: 112). The term *Proto-West Germanic* is therefore, like *Old English*, a portmanteau expression, covering a range of varieties.

1.7 A similar narrative may be offered for the pre-English period. It is usually held that English emerged from the other Germanic usages in the first three centuries AD, deriving from a group of dialects on the shores of the North Sea with common characteristics distinct from the other West Germanic usages. It is usual to refer to these dialects either as 'North Sea Germanic' or as 'Ingvaeonic', the latter being derived from the Roman term for the tribes who lived along the North Sea littoral (cf. Tacitus, *Germania*). There is considerable controversy about what is meant by an Ingvaeonic language (see Nielsen 1989, 2002, for a useful conspectus of scholarship to date); most scholars hold that core Ingvaeonic languages are English and Frisian, with Old Saxon as another possible—if more peripheral—member of the group.

1.8 If this narrative were recouched in accordance with a tree model, Proto-Ingvaeonic would form a superordinate node with Old English and Old Frisian as two coordinates (along with others). Such a model does capture a truth about the relationship between these varieties, but it is of course insufficient, since it would seem to argue for the existence of some common 'Proto-Old English' from which subsequently the dialects of English itself had diverged. Such a picture is an oversimplification. In the remainder of this chapter, we will explore (amongst other matters) the argument that Old English arose from the interaction of varieties, previously existing as near-related but distinct dialects in old Germania, which came together in England. Such interactions seem to have been commonplace in the West Germanic period, and it is therefore unsurprising that the process should have continued after these peoples had arrived in the British Isles.

1.9 In order to demonstrate this process, one sound change will be explored in detail: the set of diphthongizations known collectively as *Breaking*. However, other sound changes are also brought under review, since the interconnectedness of phenomena is one of the themes of this book. These other changes include characteristic Old Anglian developments such as *Retraction* and *Smoothing*, and also changes known as *First Fronting* (witnessed in both Old English and Old Frisian), *i-Mutation* (or 'i-Umlaut'), *Back Mutation* (or 'Back Umlaut') and *Late West Saxon Smoothing* (see Appendix 1). The chapter will conclude with an exploration of the epistemological issues raised by this exploration. (An earlier version of part of this chapter appeared as Smith 2002; see also Krygier 2004.)

2 A description of Old English Breaking

2.0 *Breaking* (or 'Fracture') is the term generally used by Anglicists to describe a process of diphthongisation whereby, between a front vowel and certain single consonants or consonant clusters, a back glide vowel developed, at first as [u], but subsequently lowered and centred to [ə]. This back vowel combined with the original front vowel to form a diphthong. The process seems to have taken place most fully in the West Saxon variety, but it is manifested to a lesser extent in other varieties as well. Breaking is fully described and illustrated in standard grammars and narratives, for instance those by Alistair Campbell (1959: 54–60), Richard Hogg (1992: 84–5), and Roger Lass (1994: 48–51). The development is usually dated to the period immediately after the arrival of the Anglo-Saxons in Britain, a dating to which we shall return.

2.1 The term *Breaking* is used differently with reference to cognate languages. The term is used to describe diphthongizations in Old Frisian and Old Norse, but these are distributed quite differently from Old English within the Frisian and Norse lexicons. Thus in Old Frisian, although there are a few similarities (e.g. Old Frisian *fiuchta* 'to fight', cf. Old English *feohtan*), Breaking is exemplified by *riucht* 'law', 'right' (cf. Old English *riht*), *siunga* 'to sing' (cf. Old English *singan*), and *thiukke* 'thick' (Old English *þicce*). The term *Breaking* is applied in Old Norse studies to two changes which are treated distinctly by Anglicists, namely, Breaking and Back Mutation. Old Norse Breaking may be exemplified by such forms as Old Icelandic *bjorn* 'bear' (cf. Old English *beorn* 'warrior', with Breaking), but also *jotunn* 'giant' (cf. Old English *eoton, eoten with Back Mutation). Old English Breaking, indeed, seems to be a distinct phenomenon, as witnessed by the divergence between cognates; compare Old English *weorþan* 'become', *weaxan* 'grow' with Old Icelandic *verða, vaxa*, Old High German *werden, wahsan*, Old Frisian *wertha, waxa*.

2.2 The process of diphthongization seems to be triggered in the environment of following back (i.e. velar, uvular) consonants and consonant clusters:

1. the fricative /x/ <h>, both on its own and in the sequence [xC], where C = any consonant (/x/-Breaking);
2. /r, l/ + following consonant (including geminate /rr, ll/), <rC>, <lC>, but not when /l/ was originally followed by /j/ (= /r/-, /l/- Breaking).

2.3 There is also a third environment, with following /w/ (/w/-Breaking). However, the evidence for /w/-Breaking is, it is held here, problematic, and it will thus be set aside in the body of this chapter.[11]

2.4 If, then, /w/-Breaking is left aside as part of a distinct process, the three principal environments for Breaking in West Saxon are /l/, /r/, /x/. The outputs from Breaking in recorded West Saxon, unless affected by subsequent sound changes, are forms which are spelled

---

[11] The question of /w/-Breaking might be better pursued in a footnote, since it is not germane to the overall argument of this chapter. That there is uncertainty about the precise process involved in diphthongisation before /w/ is indicated in Lass (1994: 49), who exemplified /w/-breaking with the form *eowu* 'ewe'; this form is, however, cited by Campbell (1959: 90, para. 211), and by Hogg (1992: 157–60, para. 5.105(1)), as an example of the later diphthongization known as Back Mutation. The view taken here is that the diphthongization ascribed to /w/-influence is better considered as distinct from the other components of Breaking and really part of the later change known as Back Mutation. It is noticeable that many examples used by the standard handbooks to illustrate /w/-Breaking are either explicable by Back Mutation or otherwise problematic; moreover, it is surely significant that /w/-Breaking fails in the environment of an [i] in the following syllable, cf. *niowul* 'prostrate' beside the by-form *niwel* (see Campbell 1959: 57, para. 148, 1959: 59, para. 154(2); Hogg 1992: 90, para. 5.24; Luick 1964: 139, para. 134). The <eo> in the form *hweowul* could also have been brought about through Back Mutation, cf. Germanic */xwexula/. Other forms traditionally used as examples of /w/-Breaking may also be excluded from consideration. *āsēowen* 'sifted' (past participle) could be accounted for by analogy with the infinitive *āsēon*, where the *ēo* is the result of /x/-Breaking (see Campbell 1959: 58, para. 153); it can be seen that a past participle *āsiwen* is also recorded. Hogg (1992: 89, para. 5.22 n.7) dismisses Old English *cnēo* < */kneu/, cf. Gothic *kniu*, from consideration; the forms *cneowe* (dative singular) etc. may be simple analogical extensions, and *þēow* would seem, from its etymology, to follow the same pattern as *cnēo* (cf. Gothic *þius*). As for Retraction before /w/ being exemplified by *clawu* 'claw', Hogg (1992: 80–1, esp. para. 5.13) has argued that /w/ was a post-vocalic environment where Ingvaeonic First Fronting failed (see 3.1, below), and thus forms like *clawu*, far from deriving from [æ] through Retraction, derive from forms which retained a back vowel and never developed a stressed front vowel [æ] in the first place.

<ea>, <eo>, e.g. *eald* 'old', *heard* 'hard', *eahta* 'eight', *seolh* 'seal', *eorl* 'noble', *feoh* 'property'. If all three environments are conceived of, quite plausibly, as in some sense 'back' environments, then a process of diphthongization seems phonetically reasonable (Lass 1994: 49), though there remains controversy about what the spellings <ea, eo> represent. It is usual to refer to these forms as 'short diphthongs', although the formulation is problematic; we will be returning to these quantitative issues in Chapter 5. For the time being the <ea, eo> forms produced by Breaking will simply be referred to as diphthongs.[12]

2.5 Breaking would seem to be a 'realizational or phonotactic development', as defined by John Wells (1982: 72–80, see Chapter 1, 2.4), but the question might be raised at this point as to whether Breaking is a sound change in the way it has been defined earlier— *a sound change has taken place when a variant form, mechanically produced, is imitated by a second person and that process of imitation causes the system of the imitating individual to change.*

2.6 The answer is supplied, in part at least, by the appearance of minimal pairs or near-pairs, albeit restricted to /rC/ environments, which arose from later developments, namely, metathesis (Hogg 1992: 303, para. 7.94) and syncopation. Metathesis yields forms in West Saxon which retain a monophthong in a Breaking environment, e.g. *ærn* 'house' (< *rænn), cf. *earn* 'eagle', while syncopation

---

[12] There is a well-known controversy about the status of these diphthongs, which remains a live issue; see White (2004) for an interesting recent discussion and a fairly comprehensive bibliography. One view, most famously put forward by Marjorie Daunt (1939) and now reasserted by David White (see especially 2004: 79), is that there were no Old English short diphthongs but that spellings such as <ea, eo> represent the vowels <ae, e, i> with the addition of diacritics to show the quality of the following consonant. My own view is that <ea, eo> are diphthongs, for reasons put forward in Michael Samuels's response to Daunt (Samuels 1952: 25–8); particularly apposite, I would argue, is the fairly frequent development from these forms of rising diphthongs in varieties of Middle English, such as Middle Kentish *yealde* 'old'. However, the question of length remains (as admitted in Samuels 1952: 24), and here White's arguments seem very strong, namely, that 'short diphthongs' are vanishingly rare in languages of the world, and thus it seems eccentric therefore to assume them for Old English. See further Chapter 5, Section 5.

of *berern* 'barn' produced the form *bern*, which contrasts with *beorn* 'warrior'. Pairs such as *stæl* 'place', *steal* 'stall' would seem also to demonstrate that <æ>, <ea> represented distinct phonemes. Breaking would therefore seem to be an example of 'split plus merger', whereby a sound derived through a realizational development merges with a sound derived in some other way; the fact that the diphthongs produced by Breaking share in subsequent developments would support this interpretation.

2.7 But one important question, never really addressed in the handbooks, remains: why did this set of sound changes happen when and where it did, and not before or after? (See further Smith 1996: 89.) In order to address this question, we need first, following the pattern or argument developed at the end of Chapter 3, to determine the date of Breaking.

3 The date of Breaking

3.0 The position of Breaking relative to other sound changes can be established by typological means. To exemplify these procedures, we might investigate the relationship between Breaking and two other developments in the Pre-Old English period: *First Fronting* and *i-Mutation*.

3.1 First fronting was discussed briefly in Chapter 2, 2.10. It is traditionally described as a development whereby $a \rightarrow æ$, except /_ C [+ nasal], [w]. The Proto-Germanic short open back vowel *a* appears as the short open front vowel *æ* in West Saxon, except in the environment of a following nasal consonant or [w] (despite Campbell 1959: 55; see Hogg 1992); thus forms such as *dæg, glæd*, with an open front vowel, appear beside *land*, with an open back vowel. i-Mutation is perhaps the most morphophonologically important of the prehistoric Old English sound changes, and its processes can be paralleled in many of the Germanic languages. The rules are as follows: V[+ back] $\rightarrow$ V[+ front]/_ $ *i, j*; V [+ front, + open] $\rightarrow$ V [+ front, + close] /_ $ *i, j*. In other words, when /i/ or /j/ stood in the following syllable, all stressed back vowels were fronted.

Examples of i-Mutation include *menn* 'men' (from Proto-Germanic *manniz*), yielding the Present-Day English distinction between *man* (singular) and *men* (plural). (For a fuller set of examples, see Appendix 1.)

3.2 The dating of Breaking in relation to these developments is based on an argument along the following lines; the forms *eald* 'old' and *ieldra* 'older' are relevant. The form *eald* seems to derive through Breaking from an earlier **æld*, with **æ* as the product of First Fronting, cf. Modern High German *alt*. The form *ieldra* derives from an earlier **ealdir-*, which provides an i-Mutation environment; *ie* is the umlaut of *ea*, not *æ* (which would have been raised to *e*, as happened to the word in Anglian dialects, yielding Present-Day English *elder*). Thus the chronological sequence First Fronting–Breaking–i-Mutation is established, a typology which remains generally accepted (though see Campbell 1959: 107–8 and references there cited). Breaking was not an ongoing process; by the late West Saxon period, it no longer took place in new, borrowed vocabulary—cf. *pæll* 'pallium' (cf. Jones 1989: 54; for Jones's other examples, though, see Campbell 1959: 162n).

3.3 As is suggested by its alternative specification ('Anglo-Frisian Brightening'), First Fronting is a change which is usually dated to the Ingvaeonic period of pre-English, before the arrival of the Anglo-Saxons in Britain, but Breaking, which is restricted to varieties of Old English and is not found in the same form in Frisian, is seen as immediately postdating *Adventus Saxonum* 'the arrival of the Saxons' (as the Anglo-Saxon invasions are commonly termed: Keynes 1999: 5–6). Breaking may therefore be considered the first 'English', as opposed to Ingvaeonic or West Germanic sound change affecting stressed vowels.

3.4 The circumstances of the Adventus Saxonum remain obscure; the phrase, which was coined by the early British historian Gildas and subsequently adopted by Bede, was used to describe a sudden, particular event in English history, but can be usefully repurposed to refer to the gradual process of settlement by Germanic peoples which characterized the late and post-Roman period in Britain. Bede's famous account of the geographical distribution of Angles in the north and east, Saxons in the south and Jutes in Kent and along the English south coast has been broadly confirmed by modern archaeological evidence, though there is evidence of less significant settlements by Frisians, Franks, and even Norwegians (Yorke 1999: 415–16 and references there cited).

3.5 The distribution of the various Germanic peoples on the eve of the Adventus Saxonum is both uncertain and controversial. However, most modern scholars agree that the Angles occupied the area in modern Denmark known as Angeln, to the north of modern Schleswig-Holstein, whereas the Saxons seem to have lived rather more to the south, in the area bordering Jade Bay, centred on the river Elbe and between the rivers Weser and Ems. This distribution is confirmed *inter alia* by the distribution of brooch types in grave goods: saucer-brooches characteristic of the Saxons appear in Southern England and in the Elbe–Jade region, whereas cruciform brooches characteristic of the Angles appear in burials in Angeln and in the English Midlands and North (see further Wilson 1981: 37ff.).

3.6 Given the principles of dialect geography, it is not therefore surprising that Anglian, though in many ways a West Germanic variety, differed from Saxon by being more like North Germanic. While still in use in the Germanic homeland, Anglian was the variety geographically nearest to the North Germanic dialects, and Anglian society evidently shared a common cultural heritage distinct from that of the Saxons. It is no coincidence that Anglian cultural sites in England, such as the Sutton Hoo ship-burial, look to Scandinavian artistic models, and that the Old English epic poem *Beowulf,* which seems to have emerged in the Anglian culture of the East Midlands, tells a trans-Baltic story linking Denmark with the land of the Geats, usually interpreted as located in what is now southern Sweden (see Hines 1984: *passim,* though see also Townend 2002).

3.7 Moreover, there is some slight intralinguistic evidence in the Old Anglian texts for an Anglian–North Germanic linguistic connection which predates the Viking invasions of the ninth century, for instance the preposition *til* for West Saxon *tō* in the Moore version of *Caedmon's Hymn,* dating from *c.*737. The verb *aron* 'are' in the tenth-century *Lindisfarne Gospels Gloss* is also perhaps of relevance; it is distinct from the Norse form—compare Old Icelandic *eru*—but clearly closer to the North Germanic pattern than the West Saxon *sind(on)*—compare Present-Day German *sind*. (See Townend 2002 for a thorough survey of English–Norse linguistic relationships during the Anglo-Saxon period.)

3.8 Since historical explanation in linguistic study depends—like (arguably) all historiography—on the observation of correspondences, it would seem that Anglian–Saxon linguistic distinctions relate at least in part to the closer placing of Anglian, during the period when the Angles still lived on the continent of Europe, to North Germanic. It would therefore seem logical to investigate whether the distinct developments with regard to Breaking in Anglian and Saxon derive from their distinct Germanic ancestries and their different original geographical locations. It is to this question that we should now turn.

4 The origins of /l/-Breaking

4.0 We might begin this section with the most obvious distinction between Anglian and Saxon: the difference between the two varieties in /l/-Breaking environments.

4.1 To illustrate the process we might trace the development of one form: West Saxon *eald* 'old', Anglian *ald*. Traditionally it has been held that both forms derive from Proto-West Germanic */ald/*, the vowel of which has been retained in Present-Day German *alt*. It was therefore held that the common ancestor of Anglian and Saxon—along with the ancestor of Old Frisian, the other main Ingvaeonic variety—underwent First Fronting: thus West Germanic */ald/* became Ingvaeonic */æld/*.

4.2 A frequent assumption is that Old English was originally a single variety which subsequently diverged into various accents and dialects: Anglian and Saxon. According to this view, Ingvaeonic */æld/* underwent Breaking in West Saxon to produce the historical *eald*, whereas in Anglian the form underwent a distinct sound change known as *Retraction* to produce *ald*. Thus the vowel in the Anglian form underwent a pendulum shift from /ɑ/ to /æ/ and then back to /ɑ/.

4.3 Recently, however, scholars have looked again at the plausibility of this pendulum shift. Richard Hogg (1992: 80–1, esp. para. 5.13), following a suggestion originally made by Bülbring (1902), has argued that, in the ancestor of recorded Old Anglian, proto-Germanic /ɑ/ failed to undergo First Fronting in the environment of a 'covered l' (i.e. /l/ + consonant).

4.4 If Hogg's view is accepted—and it is certainly plausible, not least in terms of economy—then this would suggest that the realization of /l/ in the ancestor of Anglian was markedly 'back' in quality even before the advent of First Fronting. The question then arises: is there any independent evidence for a distinct back realization of /l/ in Anglian?

4.5 As is the case when dealing with phonetic details of a language variety of such antiquity, we have to build on a mixture of small indications, including the analysis of correspondences. With regard to velar /l/, the best and most relevant evidence comes from the Present-Day Danish of east Jutland, where a velarized /l/ is still in use (see Haugen 1976: 275 and reference cited there). In more northerly Scandinavian dialects this sound eventually merged with the acoustically somewhat similar so-called 'cacuminal' or 'thick' /l/ (see Haugen 1976: 274–8); thick /l/ is usually considered to be an '/r/-like /l/' ([r, l] are of course in many languages not distinct phonemes, for example in Japanese). Haugen (976: 273) argues that a velarized /l/ was the usual realization in Pre- (i.e. pre-550 AD) and Common (550–800) Scandinavian.

4.6 It therefore seems at least possible that Anglian, the variety of West Germanic closest to North Germanic, could have developed its early velarised /l/ through contact with Pre-Scandinavian while the Angles were still living in their Germanic homeland. The velarized /l/ prevented the development of First Fronting in this environment in the ancestor of Anglian: thus the retention of *ald* /ɑld/.

4.7 This velarised /l/ moved with the Anglians during the invasions of the fifth century AD. In England, the velarised /l/—perceptually quite a significant feature—was adopted by the West

Saxons, in a situation of linguistic contact (why West Saxons should copy an Anglian form will be discussed in 7, below). But since the ancestor of West Saxon had had First Fronting, the outcome of the velarization in that variety was somewhat distinct from Anglian in terms of vocalic development.

4.8 There remains the question of Anglian forms such as *ældra* 'older', derived from **/ɑldira/*, with the i-Mutation of 'retracted' a. That /l/ has not restrained fronting due to i-Mutation suggests either that the /l/ has changed in its realization or, more probably, that the 'front' vowel-harmony effects of i-Mutation outweigh or compensate for the 'back' quality of /l/. Such mutation effects are still recorded in Present-Day English (see Wells 1982: 533–4).

5 The origins of /r/-Breaking

5.0 The question of /r/-breaking is a little more problematic. The distinct Northumbrian development of /r/-breaking, combined with the evidence of Present-Day Northumbrian dialects, would suggest that a 'back' /r/ first developed in Northumbrian varieties of Anglian, subsequently spreading—again in England—to other accents.

5.1 'Uvular r' [ʀ] develops earliest in North Germanic in Danish (see Haugen 1976: 72–3), and has spread from there into southern Sweden (on the history of /r/-realizations in Germanic, see Erickson 2002). The evidence would seem to indicate that the variety of Anglian which ultimately became Northumbrian derived its uvular realization of /r/ from the period of contact between West and North Germanic varieties. A weakened, velar form of the uvular /r/, rather akin to that found in some varieties of American English (see Lass 1983), could have been subsequently adopted by other varieties of Anglo-Saxon. Such a development would account for the early, Ingvaeonic-period failure of First Fronting in the ancestor of Old Northumbrian (producing *barnum*, etc.) beside the later, post-Ingvaeonic and post-First Fronting developments in more southerly varieties of Old English. If this hypothesis is accepted it would of course also suggest that the precursor of Old Northumbrian was developing as a variety distinct from the rest of Anglian even before the Angles left their Germanic homeland.

5.2 However, it is interesting that metathesized or syncopated forms, such as *ærn* 'house' (<*rænn*), *bern* 'barn' (<*berern*), which produced minimal pairs (see 2.6), were not subjected to breaking-type diphthongisations. This fact would suggest either that these metatheses took place after Breaking had been completed or that the conditions which triggered Breaking had ceased to be operative. One possibility, which would depend on there being a chronological gap between Breaking and metathesis, is that the realization of /r/ had lost its back quality by the time the metathesized forms developed.

5.3 Another, perhaps more likely, possibility is that the /r/ involved in metathesis was realized in a way distinct from that involved in Breaking, perhaps syllabically (as in some varieties of present-day Scandinavian, e.g. Dano-Norwegian; see Haugen 1976: 74–5), or with a glide vowel between /r/ and /n/. Such developments as the latter are frequently found as intermediate stages in some kinds of metathesis (see Samuels 1972: 16–17), and would seem a logical development of the syncopated forms as well; cf. Common Slavic *zolto* 'gold' > Russian *zoloto* (East Slavic) beside Czech *zlato* (West Slavic). As has been pointed out, the precise mechanisms involved in metathesis have received surprisingly little attention (see Jones 1989: 191, but see more recently Blevins and Garrett 1998 and references there cited for a cross-linguistic discussion).[13]

6 The origins of /x/-Breaking

6.0 The third, and most productive, Breaking environment is the fricative /x/. All varieties of Old English demonstrate breaking before /x/, and this would suggest that it was invariably realized in

---

[13] An important extension of this discussion, drawn to my attention by Krygier (2004), is Howell (1991), in which Howell presents useful evidence for the role of /r/ in breaking-like diphthongizations.

all environments, at an early date, as a 'back' velar fricative consonant, as in present-day Yiddish or Afrikaans and in some varieties of
Dutch (see Lass 1994: 75). It would thus have differed from the
modern front–back distribution seen in (e.g.) Present-Day German
hoch, Hoechst, with [x, c], respectively. Such a distinction seems to
have emerged towards the end of the Old English period, and it is
sustained by those varieties which have kept /x/ as part of their
phonemic inventory, for example the Scots distinction between
[nɔxt, nict] 'not', 'night'. However, the contrast between Old English
feoh 'property' (with Breaking) and its cognate Old High German
feho, or between Old English (West Saxon) *seah* 'saw' and its cognate
Old High German *sah*, would seem to indicate that the general
realization of /x/ <h> as a back consonant whatever the environment was an innovation in prehistoric Old English.

   6.1 Given the argument put forward so far, can we argue that
Anglian /x/ came to be realized solely as a velar (as opposed to a
palatal) fricative, after the operation of First Fronting, and that it in
turn affected the realization of West Saxon /x/? The evidence for
such an argument is again problematic, but there does seem to be a
correspondence in dating between the presumed establishment of
velar realizations of /x/ in the ancestors of Anglian and Saxon and
a redistribution of fricatives in what became Common Scandinavian
(see Haugen 1976: 155). Could the Anglian change have been
triggered by this change—and subsequently spread to West Saxon
when the two varieties came into contact after the Adventus
Saxonum? Certainly there would seem to be room for further
investigation in this area.

   6.2 However it arose, the diphthongizations were not sustained
later in the Old English period. Just before the time of historical
records, Anglian dialects underwent the development known as
Smoothing, whereby the diphthongs produced by /x/-Breaking
were monophthongized; thus Anglian had undergone the change
nēh 'near' > *nēoh* > *nēh*. Now, such pendulum shifts have already
been considered unlikely (see section 4, above), but Richard Hogg
has offered a fairly convincing explanation on prosodic grounds (see
Hogg 1992: 143–4). The result would be the rightward transfer of

'[j]-prosody' from the first (front) element of the diphthong to the following consonant, as a result of the obscuration of the second element of the diphthong, probably in [ə]. The fact that Smoothing fails in [x]-Breaking environments when a back vowel remains in the following syllable indicates that something along these lines had taken place, cf. the alternation *þuerh* 'crooked' (with /rx/-Breaking) beside *þweoran* accusative singular (Hogg 1992: 144).

6.3 The preconditions for Smoothing would seem to be two: obscuration of the second element of the diphthong, and subsequent fronting of the phoneme /x/. Something similar occurs in Late West Saxon ('Late West Saxon Smoothing', Campbell 1959: 131); this development has generally been seen as distinct from Anglian Smoothing, but it may simply be a later development of the same kind. There is some evidence that more southerly dialects of Old English and Middle English were more conservative with regard to diphthongal developments, and it may be that the obscuration of the second element of the diphthong, one of the two preconditions, took longer to develop here, and that Smoothing was therefore also somewhat delayed in consequence. (See also Hogg 1992: 101–6, esp. 1992: 103, para. 5.44, for the lowering of the second element of the diphthong produced by Breaking, which seems to be detectable earliest in Anglian.)

6.4 The outcome of the developments just discussed was that the Middle English distinction emerged between 'front vowel + front /x/' and 'back vowel + back /x/' in *knight, nought*, for example, a distinction which would only be (partially) obscured by later developments.

7 A hypothesis as to the origins of Breaking

7.0 It will be fairly obvious from the preceding discussion that much remains obscure about the origins of the Old English sound changes, including Breaking. However, it is argued here that a reasonable hypothesis as to the origins of this sound change may be put forward, while admitting freely that final proof for such a course of events will almost certainly always be lacking.

7.1   The hypothesis depends on two insights:

1. that linguistic historiography (like other historical disciplines) depends upon the careful analysis of extra- and intra-linguistic correspondences, and
2. that the interaction of varieties in present-day situations has a relevance for the understanding of past states of the language (the 'uniformitarian hypothesis').

7.2 The first of these points has been covered explicitly in the preceding argument. The second point has been made somewhat implicitly hitherto, and thus needs a little expansion. The history of Old English is often taken as the history of the emergence of 'standard' Old English, West Saxon. Yet West Saxon as we have it, it has been argued here, is really the product of an earlier interaction with Anglian, subsequent to or perhaps during the Adventus Saxonum. There is some evidence that, during the earlier phases of the Anglo-Saxon period, Anglian culture was dominant, and thus, we might expect, the Anglian variety was sociolinguistically dominant; England, after all, derives its name from the Angles and not the Saxons, and this choice seems to have been made early on. As Myres (1986: 107–8) puts it:

It has recently been suggested...that when the main tide of migration to Britain took place in the fifth century, the Angles on the Continent were already becoming the dominant element in the *Mischgruppe* of peoples pressing south-westward into Frisia from all the lands around the lower valleys of the Elbe and the Weser. There is no doubt that this southward pressure of Angles, Jutes, and related tribes was a major force behind the migration to Britain at this time. If in fact the Angles played a leading part in the movement, that might well account for the substitution of their name for that of the Saxons over so much of eastern Britain. It would mean that in the fifth century, as distinct from what happened in the fourth or third, the main impetus was now coming from what German scholars have termed the *Grossstamm der Angeln*. It would have incorporated all the restless peoples on the north German and Frisian coasts under the leadership of Angle or Jutish chieftains pressing down from Jutland, Schleswig, and the Baltic lands beyond the lower Elbe.

It is possible that the process of Anglian dominance, therefore, was already under way as the Angles and Saxons were en route to their areas of settlement.

7.3 In short, the origin of the prehistoric Old English sound changes, often treated as a rather esoteric set of formalisms, becomes explicable when seen in the context of the historically attested movement of peoples—and thus may be explained by reference to present-day observations informed by sociolinguistic theory. These sound changes may, in short, be seen as the outcome of 'H&H' processes of the kind discussed in earlier chapters.[14]

8 Implications

8.0 It was argued in Chapter 1 that language change, including sound change, depends crucially on contact. It was suggested there that the raw material for sound change always exists, in the continually created variation of natural speech, but sound change only happens when a particular variable is selected in place of another as part of systemic regulation. Such processes of selection take place when distinct systems interact with each other through linguistic contact, typically through social upheavals such as invasion, revolution or immigration; as Angus McIntosh has insisted, 'Fundamentally, what we mean by "languages in contact" is "users of languages in contact" and to insist upon this is much more than a terminological quibble and has far from trivial consequences' (1994: 137). And interestingly the set of changes known as Breaking corresponds very closely to a key moment of contact: the coming together of Anglian and Saxon varieties, during the Adventus Saxonum, to produce Anglo-Saxon.

---

[14] Similar sociohistorically informed arguments have been proposed to explain developments in other Old English dialects. Perhaps the most influential of these is that put forward with regard to Kentish in Samuels (1971), in which specifically Kentish developments are seen as relating to continuing contact between Kent and the Low Countries in the post-Adventus Saxonum period.

8.1 Scholars are paid to be sceptical, and an easy response to the hypothesis put forward here might be something as follows: Where is the proof? We know so little about this shadowy period that it is very risky to attempt any explanation at all of such events as Breaking, especially based on such a problematic body of evidence.

8.2 Such arguments can be countered along the following lines. Given that, for reasons discussed in Chapter 1, historical explanation is a valid activity, what alternative is offered? Historical explanation is an argument, and absolute proof would seem to be an impossibility: thus the practice of history is a matter of 'unfolding conversations' between different practitioners (see Curzan and Emmons 2004).

8.3 We will return to these arguments in the last chapter of this book. In the next chapter, we will investigate, from a similar perspective, developments which took place during a considerably less shadowy period, the transition between Anglo-Saxon and Norman England.

5

From Old to Middle English

1 The transition from Old to Middle English

1.0 Whereas the principal example discussed in the previous chapter dates from a very shadowy period in the history of the English language, the transition from Old to Middle English, though still in many ways problematic evidentially, is much better attested in the written record. A considerable amount of material survives from this transitional period, including important texts which offer fascinating evidence for contemporary pronunciation.

1.1 Of these, perhaps the best known is *The Ormulum*, a cycle of metrical sermons which survives in MS Oxford, Bodleian Library Junius 1, so-named *forrþi þatt Orrm itt wrohhte* 'because Orm made it'. *The Ormulum* is usually localized to Lincolnshire and dated to *c.*1200; it survives, comparatively rarely for a Middle English text, in an authorial holograph (see further Parkes 1983). Orm's 'phonetically written' spelling system, though eccentric to present-day eyes, is completely logical for the purposes for which it was devised: it seems Orm attempted, with considerable ambition, to provide a coherent transcription of contemporary pronunciation from his area and time. But recent work has shown that Orm was not, as he might appear, alone; the Early Middle English period in particular has been described as the age of 'mini-Orms' (Derek Britton, p.c.), writers who attempted to varying degrees to reorganize the writing systems they had inherited from Old English, Old French, and Latin, in order to reflect the phonological structure of the English of their area. Whereas Old English texts largely survive in Late West Saxon, a comparatively focussed form of written English which had achieved partial elaboration by the end of the Anglo-Saxon period, Middle English texts reflect in writing, to a lesser or greater degree, the variety of contemporary speech.[15]

1.2 In phonological terms, the major differences between Old and Middle English are the phonemicization of the voiced–voiceless distinction in fricatives, certain shifts in some dialects in the distribution of vowels, and certain quantitative changes. The first of these has been discussed in Chapter 3, while the second will be referred to in Chapter 6 as a contributory factor in dialectal differentiation. It is with the third of these changes, quantitative developments, that this chapter will be primarily concerned.

2 Compensatory Lengthening

2.0 The main quantitative changes which took place in English during the Old and Early Middle English periods are sometimes grouped together as varieties of *Compensatory Lengthening*. Compensatory Lengthening is a widely attested linguistic phenomenon, taking place when loss of one segment in a string of sounds is compensated for by lengthening of another, for example CVC > CVV, CVCV > CVVC, where C = consonant, V = vowel, and VV = 'long' vowel.

2.1 Perhaps the most substantial, and certainly the widest ranging, survey yet undertaken of the phenomenon is by Darya Kavitskaya (2002). Kavitskaya found that Compensatory Lengthening of the type

---

[15] A small caveat should be added here: although *The Ormulum* is an important work for the student of English historical phonology, Orm himself was not a historical phonologist, and his writing system includes features which do not reflect phonological distinctions. Thus, for instance, Orm distinguishes <ꟻh> in *leꟻhenn* 'lie', *læh* 'lied' (third-person preterite singular), but this seems to be an allophonic and not a phonemic distinction; see Fulk (1996: 485) and Burchfield (1956). For further important discussion of such issues and their implications, see Fulk (1996: *passim*) and references there cited.

CVC > CVV appears in 57 languages belonging to 18 different families of language, and she found lengthening of the type CVCV > CVVC in 21 languages 'representing five different language families' (Blevins 2004: 151).

2.2 Kavitskaya's findings were summed up recently by Juliette Blevins:

Kavitskaya (2002) . . . argues that both changes are the result of phonologization of pre-existing vowel-length differences. The general hypothesis is that Compensatory Lengthening results in cases where length, which was once attributable to phonetic factors, is no longer interpreted this way by the listener. Phonetic factors leading to vowel lengthening include longer V-C transitions for particular consonants, longer vowels before particular consonants, and open-syllable lengthening.   (Blevins 2004: 151)

In other words, Compensatory Lengthening relates to perception, and to the speaker–listener relationship; as Kavitskaya puts it, it 'originates in perceptual properties of speech' (2002: 99). Allophonically 'long' phenomena, according to this theory, develop at particular points in time a systemic function, through split, merger, or shift; Compensatory Lengthening is therefore the phonological activation of a pre-existing allophonic variant, 'a phonological reanalysis of inherent phonetic duration of vowels' (Kavitskaya 2002: 106).

2.3 Compensatory Lengthening of both kinds operates at various times in the history of English. CVC > CVV, for instance, is demonstrated by a form which also demonstrates Breaking, discussed in Chapter 4: the attested Old English forms *slēan* and *tēon* derive from reconstructed **sleahan* and **teohan*, whose stressed vowels are reflexes, with /x/-Breaking, of earlier /æ/, /e/. However, the Breaking environment is obscured by subsequent loss of medial *h* and Compensatory Lengthening of the stressed vowel, followed by assimilation of the inflectional ending in -*an*. Old English had a phonemic distinction between the sounds represented graphemically as *ea, eo* and *ēa, ēo*, even if there remains uncertainty about the existence of a short/long distinction in diphthongs (White 2004; see section 5, below). This minor redistribution of sounds within the lexicon is therefore a real sound change in terms of our working definition: *a sound change has* *taken place when a variant form, mechanically produced, is imitated by a second person and that process of imitation causes the system of the imitating individual to change.* Later examples of CVC > CVV lengthening in Old English include the contrast between Early West Saxon *sægde* and Late West Saxon *sǣde*.

3 Homorganic Lengthening

3.0 A more complex, and theoretically interesting, example of CVC> CVV is exemplified in the late Old English period by a process known as *Homorganic Lengthening*, that is, lengthening of a vowel in the environment of a following liquid or nasal plus voiced consonant pronounced using the same articulatory organs. This process may be exemplified by the change *cild* > *cīld*, where the voiced alveolar lateral /l/ is followed by the voiced alveolar plosive /d/ (cf. the diphthong in Present-Day English *child*, where the Middle English long vowel has been subjected to the Great Vowel Shift). This change did not take place when the consonant group in question was followed by a third consonant, as in the plural form *cildru* 'children' (cf. the stressed vowel in Present-Day English *children*, which has not undergone the Great Vowel Shift). In essence, in certain environments lengthening took place, with subsequent mergers between lengthened vowels and vowels already long and thus a redistribution of vowels within the lexicon. There are also sporadic instances where Homorganic Lengthening failed anyway, as in the Present-Day English distinction between *wind* (noun) and *wind* (verb), Old English *wind, windan*. This distinction may be the result of a disambiguating choice between variant pronunciations to avoid confusion between two meanings (see Samuels 1972: 142), but it also raises some interesting questions as to the origins of the development, which will be discussed further below.

3.1 A standard account of the Homorganic Lengthening in late Old English has been given by Richard Hogg (1992: 213–14):

during the [Old English] period short vowels became lengthened when followed by liquid or nasal + homorganic voiced consonant, that is *ld, rd, rl, rn, rð, rs, mb, nd, ng* . . . this can be seen as part of the . . . tendency to equalise the lengths of stress feet, in this case by the lengthening of short stressed syllables... For this to be the case it must be assumed that such consonant clusters had a special status in syllable structure, in that their behaviour was more akin to that of a single consonant than that of a bimoric cluster.

Hogg goes on to point out that the evidence for this development 'must be deduced from its interaction with other [Old English] sound changes and the fact that in [Early Middle English] vowels in these circumstances behave as long vowels'.

3.2 An insight into this development is hinted at by Hogg's reference to 'a bimoric cluster'. This term derives from moraic theory, in which the mora is a phonic 'beat', rather like a note in music, a notion developed for the analysis of syllable structure and stress-assignment. Traditionally, one mora is equivalent to a short vowel segment (V), whereas two morae are equivalent to a long vowel segment (VV). (See Kavitskaya 2002: 20–2 for a convenient overview of moraic theory.)

3.3 According to moraic theory, Homorganic Lengthening might be seen to have evolved according to the following rule: CVCC > CVVC. Either groups such as /lC, rC, nC/ (where C is a homorganic voiced consonant), hitherto seen as CC, start to be perceived as C, and the vowel V is lengthened to VV to compensate, or groups such as /Vl, Vr, Vn/ etc., hitherto seen as VC, start to be perceived as VV. Kavitskaya sees the process as relating to the fine-grain phonetics of the clusters in question: 'in certain contexts, intrinsic phonetic properties of the speech signal can be misparsed and reinterpreted, yielding phonologization' (2002: 10).

3.4 Phonetically, it is possible to see /l, r, m, n/, the first elements in such groups, as liable to dissimilation or assimilation, either to the preceding vowel or to the following consonant. If the latter is the case, then we might argue that /l, r, m, n/, being formed in the same place of articulation as the consonants which followed them and thus homorganic with them, became assimilated to these later consonants; cf. /hand-/ > [ham-] in many Present-Day English pronunciations of the word *handbag*.

3.5 In terms of manner of articulation, /l, r, m, n/ may be described as sonorants, 'sound[s] whose phonetic content is predominantly made up by the sound waves produced by [their] voicing' (Giegerich 1992: 20). /l, r, m, n/ are thus the most 'vowel-like' of English consonants, and liable to dissimilation to a preceding vowel; cf. vocalisations, such as [mɪʊk] 'milk' in many varieties of British English. (We might contrast obstruents, whose 'articulation involves an obstruction of the air stream that produces a phonetic effect independent of voicing', Giegerich 1992: 20. Obstruents include /t, p, s, z/.)

3.6 Interestingly, the development of Homorganic Lengthening is patchy in the history of English; whereas most vowels preceding /lC/ groups have retained their long vowels, fewer have retained them in the environment of following /mC/ or /nC/ groups, where /C/ is in each case a homorganic voiced consonant. The voicing is an important component: it is noticeable that, in homorganic environments in Present-Day English, there is a perceptible length difference in vowels depending on whether the final consonant is voiced or not—cf. the pairs *fort : ford* (in rhotic accents), *bolt : bold, mount : mound, lamp : lamb* (see Raphael 1972 for instrumental confirmation), and this phenomenon clearly relates to allophonic long–short differences in Present-Day English pairs such as *beat : bead, thought : thawed* (Laver 1994: 152). To sum up, the environment for Homorganic Lengthening would seem, for a number of reasons, to be a good example of a situation whose 'intrinsic phonetic properties' (to use Kavitskaya's phrase) has the potential to 'yield phonologization'.

3.7 Homorganic Lengthening is usually dated by its relationship to an earlier Old English development, i-Mutation, which was discussed in the previous chapter (see Chapter 4, 3.1 and *passim*). Under i-Mutation, *æ > e* before nasals, as in *cemban, sendan*, but *ǣ* was unaffected, and thus we would expect forms such as **sǣndan* to appear if the lengthening had preceded i-Mutation; since such forms do not appear, it is usually argued that Homorganic Lengthening did not take place before i-Mutation (see Campbell 1959: 120–1). Lengthening, however, seems to have taken place by the tenth century in West Saxon, before the change of *sel- > syl-* exemplified by Early West Saxon *self*, Late West Saxon *sylf*; this latter change does not affect long vowels, and we might note therefore the retention of the form *seldan*, suggesting that the *e* was by that time lengthened, yielding *sēldan*. (See Hogg 1992: 200 n. 2.)

3.8 Homorganic Lengthening seems certainly to have taken place by the time of *The Ormulum* (*c*.1200). Orm regularly doubled consonants after short vowels, as in unstressed words such as *wollde* 'would', *annd* 'and'; the concomitant implication is that single consonants, as in *ald*(*e*) 'old', *wendenn* 'turn', 'go' indicate a preceding long vowel. Orm also demonstrates the restriction on the development when a third consonant follows, as in *hand* 'hand', *hanndlenn* 'handle' (verb). (See Hogg 1992: 200 n. 2; Fulk 1996: 482; for reservations as to the relative chronology of Homorganic Lengthening and Open Syllable Lengthening, see Ritt 1994: 92–3, though Ritt does not take account of the *seldan* example.)

4 Middle English Open Syllable Lengthening: description

4.0 It has been argued (notably by Minkova 1982) that Kavitskaya's other category of Compensatory Lengthening, CVCV > CVVC, can be exemplified for English by another change, *Middle English Open Syllable Lengthening*; this claim will be discussed here.

4.1 Early in the thirteenth century, most scholars agree, the short vowels *a*, *e*, and *o*, which by this time were qualitatively [a, ɛ, ɔ], were lengthened in so-called open syllables of disyllabic words when the peak and coda of the unstressed syllable was either -*eø* or -*en*, as in Old English *beran* > Middle English *bēre*(*n*) 'bear' (= verb), Old English *macian* > Middle English *māken* 'make', Old English *þrote* > Middle English *þrōte* 'throat'. It will be observed that in all these examples the unstressed syllable has been lost in Present-Day English. Lengthening often failed in those words where the unstressed syllable has not been lost, as in *penny*, *radish*, *body*, *gannet* (cf. Old English *penig*, *radisc*, *bodig*, *ganot*), but compare *cradle* (from Old English *cradol*) beside Present-Day English dialectal *creddle*, *naked* (from Old English *nacod*). The development seems to have taken place a little earlier in Northern Middle English.

4.2 Later, or so it is generally held, in the late thirteenth (northern) and fourteenth (southern) centuries, *i* and *u* also underwent lengthening to *ē*, *ō* respectively, as in Old English *wicu* > Middle English *weke* 'week', Old English *wudu* > Middle English *wode* 'wood'; that Middle English had a long vowel in these words is flagged by the Present-Day English <ee>-, <oo>-spellings. This development seems to have operated differently from the earlier one, in that it affected words where the unstressed syllable remains in Present-Day English, for example *evil, beetle, weevil* (see Fulk 1996; Minkova 1982). Middle English Open Syllable Lengthening did of course fail to affect a few words where it might have been expected to have manifested itself, for instance *sunu* 'son', *lufu* 'love'. The failure of such forms to undergo lengthening is traditionally associated with early loss of final -*e*. (See Jordan 1974: 63, §36.3; 66, §38.3.)

4.3 One implication of all these developments is that the short vowels were closer in quality in the late Old English period than they became in Early Middle English. <i>-spellings in *cīld*, derived from Homorganic Lengthening, beside unlengthened *i*, spelled <i>, in *cildru*, contrast with <e(e)>-spellings in *wēke*, where the *ē* derived from Middle English Open Syllable Lengthening seems to be the reflex of Old English *i* in *wicu*. Lengthened forms of [ɪ, ʊ], [ɪː, ʊː], would have merged with the reflexes of Old English *ē/ēo*, and *ō* respectively. As Ladefoged and Maddieson (1996: 285–6) point out, [ɪː, ʊː] and [eː, oː] are acoustically very close, and mergers are to be expected. It is no surprise therefore that <e, o> were used as the spellings for both 'original' long vowels and those long vowels which resulted from Middle English Open Syllable Lengthening. It is also no surprise that, conversely, when the Old English vowels *ē*, *ēo* underwent sporadic shortening, they merged with /ɪ/ and shared in its subsequent history, e.g. Old English *sēoc* 'sick'.

4.4 The relationship between lowering and lengthening is a complicated one; it seems likely that the quality of the short vowels varied dialectally, with closer realizations in southern varieties and more open ones in the North and Midlands. The lengthening of *i, u*, moreover, is comparatively restricted, and seems to have begun in the North. It is noticeable that the examples used in the standard handbooks are in many cases of problematic etymology (for notes on these forms, see Appendix 2). We will be returning to the implications of this development in 5, below.

4.5 It has been traditionally held that Middle English Open Syllable Lengthening had not occurred in Orm's language. This view is supported by an observation about Orm's prosodic practice. Orm has two kinds of line: four-beat (e.g. *Annd Sannte Marʒess time wass*) and three-beat (e.g. *ðatt ʒho þa shollde childenn*). At the end of his three-beat lines, Orm has a restricted range of usages: he uses disyllables with short vowels in closed root-syllables and long vowels, and long vowels in all kinds of syllables. However, he never uses disyllables where a long vowel was to result from Middle English Open Syllable Lengthening; thus *takenn* (from Old English *tācn* 'sign') appears at the end of a three-beat line, but never *takenn* ('take', 'taken'). Orm seems to have made the distinction clear by the use of a special diacritics on vowels in open syllables, doing so because 'this is the only place at which Orm's system of ortho-graphic geminates leaves the vowel quantity ambiguous' (Fulk 1996: 487). (An attempt has been made to revisit Orm's metrical use, but the examples adduced are problematic; see Phillips 1992, but also the response in Fulk 1996: 488–90.)

4.6 Donka Minkova (1982) has argued that Middle English Open Syllable Lengthening is a process of Compensatory Lengthening, whereby loss of -*e*(*n*) is compensated for by lengthening of the stressed vowel and suggesting that the tendency for lengthening to fail when the unstressed syllable ends in a consonant supports this analysis. Aditi Lahiri and Elan Dresher (1999) have disputed this claim, noting that Open Syllable Lengthening in all environments is characteristic of other Germanic languages at roughly the same time, and suggesting an alternative prosodic explanation. The com-parative evidence is interesting, though of course not conclusive: it is quite possible for languages to arrive at similar outcomes for differ-ent reasons. It seems that the question as to whether Compensatory Lengthening operated in Middle English Open Syllable Lengthening is connected closely to the plausibility of the explanation for the phenomenon.

5 Quantitative changes from Old to Middle English: an historical explanation

5.0 The two phenomena just described, Homorganic Lengthening (and concomitant shortening) and Middle English Open Syllable Lengthening, have often been seen as linked attempts to sustain isochronicity, in other words, as regularly timed intervals between prominent or stressed elements in the spoken chain. Such an explanation underpins Hogg's comment already cited, '[Homorganic Lengthening] can be seen as part of the...tendency to equalise the lengths of stress feet, in this case by the lengthening of short stressed syllables...' (1992: 213).

5.1 We know, from the analysis of Old English verse, that stressed syllables were generally 'long', something characteristic of many languages (see Blevins 2004: 13 and references there cited). That is, their rhyming component consisted of a long vowel followed by a single consonant (VVC), e.g. *stān* 'stone', or a short vowel followed by two consonants (VCC), e.g. *storm* 'storm'. By a process known as *Resolution*, the sequence 'short vowel–single consonant–short vowel' (VCV) seems also to have been regarded as an acceptable equivalent to the long syllable, as in *nama* 'name'. (See further Hogg 1992: 210–14, and references cited there.)

5.2 However, as we have seen, length or shortness in syllabic structure was not, it would appear, fixed in the history of English. Homorganic Lengthening would seem to indicate one such disturbance, and Middle English Open Syllable Lengthening another. Kavitskaya argues that such lengthenings, always potentially possible, are activated in accordance with Blevins's formulation when perceived as such by the listener, and this perceptual element, which might be deemed as to do with contrast, fits rather well with our working definition of sound change: *a sound change has taken place when a variant form, mechanically produced, is imitated by a second person and that process of imitation causes the system of the imitating individual to change.* A series of questions arise, however, notably: Why then? What are the contingent circumstances which produced this event in this time and place, and not before, given that the phonetic conditions for the development were present throughout the period when the cluster existed? Are these developments, which seem to take place (*pace* Ritt 1994: *passim*) at different times, in some way connected?

5.3 Part of the answer to these questions with reference to both changes might lie in the general phonetic context in which the lengthening took place. According to Hogg, there are various processes of lengthening and shortening which took place late in the Old English period, and all these changes 'shared a common feature, in that all were dependent upon Old English syllable structure and stress patterns. Essentially these changes appear to have occurred in order to approximate as far as possible to isochronous intervals between stressed syllables' (Hogg 1992: 210). Lengthening might therefore be expected as part of a consequent attempt to sustain isochrony not just within syllables but between syllables; it thus relates to the prosodic structure of the language.

5.4 The most obvious candidate as the source for this development is the reduction and eventual loss of unstressed syllables which characterized the late Old English and Early Middle English periods, and which introduced a major change in English prosody: a major reorganization of the relationship between the language's rhythmical structure, expressed (like verse) in feet, and its word forms. This development, found to a greater or lesser extent in all the Germanic (and many other Indo-European) languages, may be characterised as a 'drift' or long-term tendency; it is usually related to the fixing of stress on initial syllables which took place in Germanic after the operation of Verner's Law. The reduction and loss of unstressed syllables, in moraic theory, would require the reassignation of the lost mora(e) in order to sustain isochronicity. This reduction of distinctions between vowels in unstressed syllables may be characterised as follows: a '(full) V' becomes a '(reduced) v', rather like, in music, a crotchet becoming a quaver in a bar, and another crotchet being dotted to compensate. Comparable reduced phenomena are found in many languages, such as the 'jers' characteristic of varieties of Slavonic, and have been described as 'weakened' forms by a number of students of Germanic languages (see Haugen 1976: 260). Such a development probably underpins the change from trochaic to iambic phrase stress in the history of English, whereby 'stem + inflection' phrases were replaced by 'unstressed determiner/ auxiliary + stem' phrases (see Smith 1996: 158–9 and references there cited for further discussion of this development).

5.5 Here, Nikolaus Ritt's work on Quantity Adjustment (1994) is relevant. Ritt, whose approach draws extensively on moraic theory, relates the change to suprasegmental developments deriving from inflectional obscuration and loss. Ritt also links Homorganic Lengthening to another change in the history of English—Middle English Open Syllable Lengthening—and sees the processes as deriving from similar triggers. However, this explanation cannot be the whole story. The difference in date between the various phenomena remains (despite Ritt's gallant attempts to link the phenomena, 1994: *passim*), and this would suggest that the precise circumstances of origin for each development differed. For this reason, quantitative changes in the transition from Old to Middle English will be divided into three sets, as follows:

  a. Homorganic Lengthening;
  b. Shortening;
  c. Middle English Open Syllable Lengthening.

5.6 (a) *The origins of Homorganic Lengthening.*   Perhaps the best-known contrastive word pair illustrating Homorganic Lengthening is *child : children,* Old English *cild : cildru.* A prosodic explanation for this development might run as follows: *cild > cīld* in order to sustain the prosodic pattern whereby stress is placed on heavy syllables, so CVCC > CVVC. The key development would seem to be in the nature of the consonant cluster: something caused the cluster to be treated as C whereas once it was treated as CC and CVC is not an acceptable heavy syllable. However, this development is unnecessary with *cildru,* since the sequence would still be an acceptable stressed unit under Resolution: CVCCV > CVCV. This pattern, it might be argued, has been sustained into Present-Day English in this word, because of the adoption (rather rarely) of the weak-noun *-an* marker for plurals.

However, the lengthening *cild* > *cīld* cannot be the result of inflectional loss, since, in recorded Old English, there was no inflection to lose in this form, and this fact would argue against the process as being to do with prosodic factors.

5.7 One possible explanation, based on the modern phonetic evidence, is that the nature of the final consonant has changed. All the continental West Germanic languages have had a tendency to devoice final plosives; thus a Middle High German development is final-consonant devoicing, yielding pairs such as *Tac* 'day', *Tage* 'days' (see Russ 1978: 65, also Keller 1978: 276). There is sporadic evidence for similar final-consonant devoicing in Old English, often if not always in the environment of a preceding /n, l, r/, witnessed by spellings like *sint* 'are' for *sind*, *færelt* 'journey' for *færeld* (see Jordan 1974: 183, who refers to /n, l, r/ as 'absorb[ing] the voicing'). The spellings are sporadic but comparatively widespread dialectally in both stressed and unstressed positions, occurring in (for instance) texts such as the *Leiden Riddle* (Northumbrian, ninth century) *ðrēt* 'thread', the *Kentish Glosses* (tenth century), *þinc* 'thing', and the *Ruthwell Cross Inscription* (Northumbrian, probably eighth century) *cyninc* 'king', etc. (see further Campbell 1959: 181–2, Hogg 1992: 287). It should be noted, though, that final devoicing is not a feature of North Germanic varieties.

5.8 By Middle English times, however, forms such as *lomp* 'lamb' are characteristic largely, though not exclusively, of the West Midlands dialect, which was a comparatively conservative variety. We might note, for instance, the forms *lomp* and *lomb* for 'lamb' in the late-fourteenth-century Middle English *Pearl*, which includes the punning lines *þe self God watz her lombe-lyȝt,/ þe Lombe her lantyrne, wythouten drede* (Gordon 1953: 38, 1045–6). Interestingly, these West Midland usages arise in stressed syllables whereas, in other dialects, final devoicing seems to be sustained only in unstressed position. If these were relic forms in Old English, as opposed to innovations, it might suggest that the <d>-spelling in Old English *cild* in West Saxon represented a devoiced pronunciation of /d/; the West Saxon spelling would therefore mask the difference in the same way as it is masked in Present-Day German spelling (cf. *Tag, Tage,* cited in Russ 1978: 65). A devoiced /d/, though distinct from a voiceless /t/, would be liable to reinterpretation as /t/: thus the sporadic spellings. Such a development would not affect *cildru*, where the syllable break would appear to take place thus: *cil* + *dru*. It may be observed that in such circumstances the medial consonant has a tendency to be assigned to the second rather than the first syllable.

5.9 If final-consonant devoicing in stressed vowels is recessive in early English, this would suggest that it was being replaced by a voiced sound. It seems at least plausible that this development occurred because English had a system where final consonants in such environments were becoming voiced. As Anglian, the most North-Germanic-like of the Old English varieties, increasingly dominated late Old English patterns of pronunciation despite the retention of West Saxon spelling practices, we would expect voiced forms to replace devoiced ones, with concomitant lengthening of vowels. This would correlate with the evidence: Hogg (1992: 287, para. 7.65 n. 2) notes that 'devoicing of final stops is more prevalent in [Early West Saxon] than in [Late West Saxon], but the discrepancy is unexplained'. Although this is highly speculative, if the devoicing were the result of the impact of North Germanic-style pronunciation on a more West-Germanic variety, an explanation would be possible.

5.10 The outcome of this conditioned lengthening would be a syllable with the rhyming element VVCC, with an extra mora. Since liquids and nasals are the most 'vowelly' of the consonants, they were liable to assimilation with the preceding long vowel, yielding VVC, and such developments would be encouraged by the foot shape of the language. It is thus possible to reconcile the prosodic and phonetic explanations for the phenomenon.[16]

---

[16] This explanation might be of interest for students of the 'quantity'-debate with regard to vowels produced by Breaking (see ch. 4, 2.4, note). Is <ea> the equivalent not, as most handbooks have it, of V, but of a long vowel VV, which is (after all) what has been presumed to result from Homorganic Lengthening? If Anglian had a tendency to voiced final consonants, then we might presume early lengthening of groups such as *ald, ard* = VVCC > VVC with assimilation of the first consonant; West Saxon *eald, eard* would be similar, with VVCC = <eaCC> = <eald, eard> > VVC <eaC>. /x/-Breaking would raise distinct problems, but loss of /x/, with Compensatory Lengthening,

5.11 (b) *Shortening.* Two kinds of Shortening are traditionally ascribed to the transition between Old and Middle English: shortening before multiple and long consonants, and shortening before trisyllabic words. However, this categorization brings together a wide range of phenomena which should probably be kept distinct.

5.12 Shortening before non-Homorganic Consonant Groups is traditionally described as a feature of late Old English, for example, late Old English *cēpte* > *cepte* 'kept', *wīfmann* > *wifmann* 'woman'; however, these examples may represent distinct phenomena. For the shortening *cēpte* > *cepte* a prosodic explanation seems very probable. In developments such as *cēpte* > *cepte* the shortening possibly relates to the obscuration of the unstressed syllable, which would have been pronounced as a sound roughly equivalent to the 'jer' of Slavonic languages; as suggested in 5.4, a distinction between 'lost' and 'weakened' unstressed vowels might be made (see Haugen 1976: 260). There would be a consequent reassignment of the consonant beginning the second syllable to the end of the preceding syllable, and the stressed syllable became 'over-long'—that is VVC + CV. Paradigmatic variation resulted, for example the Present-Day English distinction between the vowels in *keep* (cf. Old English *cēpan*) and *kept* (cf. late Old English *cepte*).

5.12 The form *wīfmann* came about through linking of two words together; in this instance, *wīfmann* 'woman', 'female human' originally contrasted with *wǣpnedmann* 'man', 'male human', and seems to have been pronounced much as the Present-Day English noun phrase *black bird*, consisting of an adjective *black* and a distinct noun *bird*. It appears that forms such as *wīfmann* came to be pronounced more as the Present-Day English compound noun *blackbird*; this development resulted in an over-long foot, and shortening took place. It seems quite

is widely attested in the history of English and, given Kavitskaya's formulation, we would expect the phenomenon to be the phonologization of a previous allophone with /x/-loss. For a discussion of the problems of 'short diphthongs', see White (2004), which is one of the most stimulating contributions to the debate yet published. Michael Samuels (1952: 24) raised some time ago the notion of the 'half-long' vowel, viz. [V.] as opposed to [V:] as relevant, and this possibility would repay further reinvestigation along the cross-linguistic lines developed by David White.

likely that such shortening could happen at any time, relating to the semantic development of the form in question.

5.13 Shortening also took place in trisyllabic words, as in *superne* 'southern', *laferce* 'lark', *haligdæg* 'holiday' (< *sūperne, lāferce, hālig-dæg*), again presumably for prosodic reasons relating to the reduction of unstressed syllables; endings such as *-ne, -ce*, and morphemes which were in origin separate words, such as *dæg*, start in unstressed situations to be assigned to the earlier foot, which becomes as a result over-heavy.

5.14 There seems to be no clear date for this last development, and it is likely that it could have happened at various times in the history of the language, largely depending on when any secondary stress was lost; it is probably best to see all these developments as sporadic developments within an overall prosodic pattern rather than the result of some general change. Thus forms such as *cēpte, sūperne*, and *lāferce* were probably shortened during the late Old English period, given that they seem to be related to the weakening of final *-e*. Shortenings of the *wīfmann > wifmann* type were probably possible at any time. Jordan (1974: 44) ascribes shortening to the late Old English period, but Hogg (1992: 214, para. 5.205) indicates that it 'was already operative at the time of the earliest texts'; Hogg's view probably applies to the latter set of changes, while Jordan's does to the former.

5.15 (c) *Middle English Open Syllable Lengthening.* The ultimate outcome of Middle English Open Syllable Lengthening can be characterized prosodically as a development whereby CVCV > CVVC, as in Old English *nama* 'name' > Middle English *nām*, Old English *faran* 'go', 'fare' > Middle English *fār*, but this outcome was some time coming, and was probably via intermediate stages such as [na.mə, fa.rən], which stages may be characterized as CVvCv(C). It would appear that forms such as *nama, faran*, which would count as resolved elements in Old English prosody, became metrically defective because the vowels in the unstressed syllables became weakened: it can therefore be argued that a Compensatory Lengthening of the stressed vowel followed.

5.16 Whether Middle English Open Syllable Lengthening can be classed as a Compensatory Lengthening is somewhat controversial.

Kavitskaya, following Lahiri and Dresher (1999), suggests that it is distinct from the compensatory processes she discusses (2002: 116). Lahiri and Dresher (1999: 715) claim

that the shared reason for [Open Syllable Lengthening] was an endeavor to maintain and maximize the Germanic foot, which was present from the oldest stages of the Germanic languages. [Open Syllable Lengthening] did not fundamentally change the earlier foot structure; rather, it contributed in different ways in the three languages to sustain the metrical pattern of the Germanic foot, in spite of other contradictory changes.

Lahiri and Dresher's article is a very significant contribution to the debate, notably in its wealth of cross-linguistic detail, and this formulation would fit well with the discussion of the actuation put forward here. But the formulation is perhaps a problematic one if seen as an argument for treating the phenomenon as non-compensatory. 'Maintaining and maximising' would seem to be broadly synonymous with 'compensating', even if there is a distinction between Middle English Open Syllable Lengthening and the other CVCV > CVVC changes which Kavitskaya discusses.

5.17 It is worth noting that Middle English Open Syllable Lengthening emerged earliest in the north of England where final -*e* was lost very early during the transition from Old to Middle English, as witnessed by spellings in the tenth-century *Lindisfarne Gospels Gloss*. In these areas, of course, inflectional endings were most thoroughly obscured first as the result of interaction between Norse and Anglian, and it may not be chance that Middle English Open Syllable Lengthening—though obviously part of a general 'drift' in the Germanic languages—corresponds in date with other likely Norse-influenced innovations such as the fronting of mid and open long back vowels (see Chapter 6, section 4). Both phenomena could relate to the break-up of tightly knit communities which seems to have accompanied the spread of 'Norsified' culture northwards and southwards from the original focal area of Viking settlement. It might therefore be argued, plausibly, that Middle English Open Syllable Lengthening was the result of a metrical development encouraged through linguistic contact between English and Norse, and triggered by inflectional weakening and loss.

5.18 As was flagged in 4.1, above, the process of lengthening seems to have taken place in two phases: an earlier phase in which *a, e, o* were lengthened, and a later phase in which lengthening of *i, u* took place. It has been argued that lengthening of *i, u* was delayed because close vowels seem to resist lengthening (see Jones 1989: 114); a prerequisite for this lengthening would, then, be a lowering of the vowel. This cannot be the whole explanation, since it would therefore be logical to suggest that lengthenings such as *cild* > *cīld* would have been resisted (which they were not); it may be, however, that Homorganic Lengthening was a stronger force than Open Syllable Lengthening, since it involved not simply metrical considerations but issues to do with the phonetics of the contributing consonant cluster. It is worth noting in this connection that, even in Present-Day English, vowels in the North tend to be realized phonetically as more open in quality than in the South (Wells 1982: 356); this fact might account for the reluctance of *i, u* to undergo Lengthening in the ancestor of the Present-Day Southern English reference accent, Received Pronunciation. As indicated in Appendix 2, only a few examples showing Open Syllable Lengthening of *i, u* exist in Received Pronunciation, and these examples have alternative etymological derivations.

5.19 In support of this last point, it may be noted that there is some evidence that, in London, Middle English short *e, o*, vowels liable to undergo Middle English Open Syllable Lengthening but otherwise comparatively stable in realization in the history of English, were realized as a pair of intermediate vowels, half-way between mid-open and mid-close. In some dialects outside London, these vowels rhymed with the reflexes of Old English *ēa/ǣ* and *ā*, respectively. Thus, in the text *On god ureisun of ure lefdi* in MS London, British Library Cotton Nero A.xiv, the following rhymes appear: *reade* 'red' (Old English *rēad*): *iureden* 'injure' (Old English *gewerdan* with metathesis), *ore* 'mercy' (Old English *ār*): *uorloren* 'lost entirely' (Old English *forloren*). This text seems to have been composed in an East Midland dialect though surviving in a manuscript from the West Midlands.

5.20 However, it seems that Chaucer, in the late fourteenth century, distinguished carefully between lengthened vowels and the reflexes of

Old English *ēa/ǣ*, *ā*, as witnessed by this stanza from his tragic poem *Troilus and Criseyde* (Book V, lines 22ff.). In this stanza, *loore* 'teaching' and *more* 'more' (with reflexes of Old English *ā*) are kept distinct from *forlore* 'lost entirely', *more* 'root', and *tofore* 'before', all of which have Old English *o* with Middle English Open Syllable Lengthening:

> *This Troilus, withouten reed or loore,*
> *As man that hath his joies ek forlore,*
> *Was waytyng on his lady evere more*
> *As she that was the sothfast crop and more*
> *Of al his lust or joies heretofore.*
> *But Troilus, now far-wel al thi joie,*
> *For shaltow nevere sen hire eft in Troie!*
>   (Benson 1988: 560)

Supporting evidence for such a distinction is supplied by Early Modern English writers on pronunciation, which indicates that Old English *e*, *o* were realized as a pair of intermediate vowels, half way between mid-open and mid-close. Thus Fausto Cercignani (1981: 60) would interpret the evidence of the early phonetician Robert Robinson as implying that Middle English /ɛ/ could be realized at the beginning of the seventeenth century as [ɛ̝] in prestigious speech, a sound roughly comparable with its reflex in Present-Day English Received Pronunciation. Lengthened [ɛ̝], i.e. [ɛ̝:] would be a sound distinct from [ɛ:]. (As will be seen in Chapter 6, this distinction has implications for a further development in the history of English sounds, namely, the Great Vowel Shift.)

5.21 Middle English Open Syllable Lengthening, therefore, seems to have been actuated by prosodic developments, originating in the north (where loss of final -*e* was earliest) and becoming more widely adopted as it moved south. In some varieties the lengthening entailed a merger with other long vowels and thus a sound change according to our definition. In others, such as London Middle English, lengthened *e* and *o* were allophones of short *e* and *o* until the loss of final -*e* in the early fifteenth century brought about a phonemicization of lengthened *e*, i.e. [ɛ̝:] > /ɛ̝:/. Middle English Open Syllable Lengthening is thus a good example of a processual sound change, one which emerged slowly, with diatopic and diachronic variation.[17]

6 Implications

6.0 It is possible, therefore, to see both Homorganic Lengthening and Middle English Open Syllable Lengthening as explicable in terms of the changing phonetic and phonological circumstances of the language at particular points in time. Both are 'real' sound changes, resulting in new phonemes, mergers, and redistributions of sounds within the lexicon, thus correlating with the working definition of sound change which is presented in this book: *a sound change has taken place when a variant form, mechanically produced, is imitated by a second person and that process of imitation causes the system of the imitating individual to change.*

6.1 However, it is of theoretical interest that both sound changes can plausibly be seen as emerging from phonetic variants. These sound changes, therefore, are emergent phenomena, and can be explained effectively within the context of an H&H model of language change; the contingent factors relate to what Blevins describes as CHOICE within a dynamically changing phonological environment.

6.2 In the next chapter, which is concerned with developments spanning the Middle and Early Modern periods, these processes will again be relevant.

---

[17] On 'imperfect lengthening' and the different outputs from Middle English Open Syllable Lengthening, see Dobson (1962) and references cited there.

6

From Middle to Early
Modern English

1 Great Vowel Shifts?

1.0 Students of English historical phonology have traditionally
focussed on the evolution of the 'standard' accents of the language:
the 'single-minded march toward R[eceived] P[ronunciation]', as
Roger Lass has called it (Lass 1976: xi). Nowhere has this focus been
more apparent than in discussions of the origins and development
of the *Great Vowel Shift*, the process of raisings and diphthongizations which distinguishes the phonologies of late Middle English
from those of the Early Modern English period and which, like all
shifts, may be described as a redistribution of sounds within the
lexicon. Almost all studies and standard handbooks dealing with
the Shift have concentrated on the area where it developed most
fully, namely, the southern parts of England, specifically London
(e.g. Baugh and Cable 1993: 232–4, though see 233 n. 1).

1.1 However, as several scholars have pointed out, the evolution
of the Shift varied diatopically, and also quite possibly diachronically, in terms of its overall shape and even actuation (see, most
accessibly, Lass 1984: 126–9 and references there cited; see also
Samuels 1972: 145). As well as a 'full' Shift affecting both the long
front and long back vowels of Middle English, characteristic
of southern varieties, there was also a distinct Shift, affecting
primarily long front vowels, which is found in northern accents.

The two Shifts are outlined schematically in Figures 6.1 and 6.2. For simplicity, they will be referred to henceforth as the Southern and Northern Shifts, respectively.

1.2 The origins of the Great Vowel Shift—or, as I would prefer, Shifts—have, notoriously, been regarded by many scholars as 'mysterious' (Pinker 1994: 250), an adjective which would seem to close down discussion. However, an interest in the origins of the Shifts has persisted, particularly amongst scholars whose work engages with sociolinguistic concerns, and it is within this tradition that the following chapter is written. It also draws specifically upon insights developed in the previous chapter, though the general themes of the book are, obviously, returned to throughout.

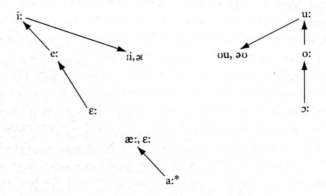

FIGURE 6.1 The Great Vowel Shift in southern England (traditional model, after Smith 1996: 87)

Note: * = output of /a/ with English Open Syllable Lengthening, phonemicized through loss of final -*e*.

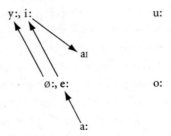

FIGURE 6.2 The Great Vowel Shift in northern England and southern Scotland (traditional model, after Smith 1996: 100)

1.3 The Shifts took place at a key moment of transition in the history of English, when it ceased to be a language of comparatively low status in comparison with Latin and French and began to take on national roles, that is to say that it underwent a process which Einar Haugen has referred to as 'elaboration' (cf. Hudson 1980: 32–4). The elaboration of English meant that prestigious varieties of that language would begin to emerge, and the story of at least one of the Shifts relates intimately to that emergence.

2 The Southern Shift

2.0 The origins of the Southern Shift have been much debated, though a consensus now seems to be emerging. Elsewhere, and drawing upon this work, I have offered a sociolinguistically informed argument for the origins of the Shift. For an earlier outline of aspects of this argument, readers are referred to Smith (1996: ch. 5), but a version tied more closely to the themes of the current book, and with some significant revisions and clarifications, may be offered here. Essentially, I argue that the Southern Shift derives from sociolinguistically driven interaction in late medieval/early Tudor London, whereby socially mobile immigrant groups hyperadapted their accents in the direction of usages which they perceived as more prestigious. Such a process can be paralleled in modern situations, whereby linguistic innovation is located in the usage of those who are weakly tied to their social surroundings.

2.1 It may be observed that the origins of the Southern Shift correspond in date to four major—and, I would argue, linked—developments in the external and internal history of the English language. These developments are as follows:

2.2 (a) *The rise of a standardized form of English.* At the end of the fourteenth and the beginning of the fifteenth centuries, it is possible to detect, in the written mode and to a much lesser extent in speech, the emergence of focussed forms of language which are the precursors of Present-Day 'standard' varieties. The development underpinning this process was the use of the vernacular in national rather than parochial situations for purposes such as, in writing, documentary record and literary expression (in the broadest sense), and, in the spoken mode, the use of English in parliament and amongst the higher echelons of society, in preference to varieties of French which had hitherto been regarded as prestigious. It was possible to be eloquent and dignified in the vernacular, a development which was paralleled at very roughly the same time in other European languages (cf. the Italian poet Dante's *On the eloquence of the vulgar tongue*, which was written, albeit in Latin, in the middle of the fourteenth century).

2.3 It should be noted—a point which will be referred to later—that French continued to occupy an important function within English society. In order to make social distinctions clear, those seeking to develop a prestigious form of the vernacular took to studding their English writing and (presumably) speech with loan-words from French. It seems likely that such words were still pronounced in a 'French manner', as witnessed by certain practices in Chaucer's verse. However, this development seems to represent a form of 'language death'; as is well known, in such situations the dying language (in this case French) throws off vocabulary into the successor language (in this case English). It is no coincidence that the great influx of Central French vocabulary into English seems to have taken place in the fourteenth and fifteenth centuries.

2.4 Standardization of writing and speech was by no means a straightforward process, as is demonstrated by the very substantial literature on the subject (e.g. Dobson 1969, Samuels 1989a, Benskin 2004, to select only three key articles). But two points might be made: it seems to have begun to emerge, albeit uncertainly, at roughly the time of the Southern Vowel Shift; and the forms which underpin modern standard usage derive from those current in late medieval London.

2.5 (b) *The growth of London.* The reasons for a London focus for standardization in writing and speech are fairly clear: the end of the Middle Ages saw the increasing significance of London as England's major administrative and trading centre. From the fourteenth century onwards there was a major influx of immigration into the capital from the countryside as folk sought to improve their condition in the city. This is, in short, the age of the quasi-mythical figure of Dick Whittington, who moved to London, where the streets were (it was said) paved with gold, to make his fortune. The result was that London became, according to contemporaries, the only English city comparable in size and importance to continental centres such as Paris, Venice, and Rome (see, for a convenient account, Ackroyd 2000 and references therein). As the story of Whittington suggests, these incomers came to dominate London polity; in the Tudor and Stuart periods, their vernacular culture provided writers such as William Shakespeare with their main audiences.

2.6 The growth of London, as in comparable situations elsewhere, had an effect on the society which looked towards it, that is, the so-called 'gravity effect' whereby a large conurbation affects the surrounding countryside. Moreover, London society, which (as nowadays) attracted incomers from elsewhere eager to take advantage of the opportunities it had to offer, may be characterized as one with weak social ties in comparison with those which obtained in the much more stable, less dynamic village society which existed elsewhere in England.

2.7 (c) *The loss of final -e*. Intralinguistically, the Southern form of the Great Vowel Shift may be dated to a grammatical development of considerable prosodic significance: the development of what is essentially the Present-Day English grammatical system with the loss of inflexional *-e*. Final *-e* was still in use in, for example, adjectival inflections in Chaucer's time, as established (*inter alia*) by the poet's verse practices, but the generations which followed Chaucer, from the end of the fourteenth century onwards, no longer recognized the form. This development is indicated by the repurposing of written *-e*: first as a decorative flourish in handwriting, added indiscriminately at the end of words without phonic significance; then used by the early printers from the end of the fifteenth century as a 'filler' letter, added to the end of words in order to assist the justification of right-hand margins; and finally, as in Present-Day English spelling, as a diacritic mark, indicating a distinct pronunciation of the letter before the intervening consonant (as in *tile*, cf. *till*).

2.8 The loss of -*e* had major implications for the pronunciation of English, whose core vocabulary became characterized as to a large extent monosyllabic in comparison with other major European languages. It also had an effect on the phonological structure of some varieties, a point to which we shall turn next.

2.9 (d) *Phonemicization of vowels affected by Middle English Open Syllable Lengthening in those accents where these vowels did not undergo merger.* This development was a consequence of the loss of final -*e*. There is good evidence, from contemporary rhyming practice in verse, that the comparatively prestigious form of speech represented by that of Geoffrey Chaucer, for instance, distinguished carefully between the reflex of Old English *e* and *o* which had undergone Middle English Open Syllable Lengthening, and the reflex of Old English *ēa*, *ǣ*; with the loss of final -*e*, this distinction became phonemicized in this variety and thus perceptually salient (see ch. 5, 5.15–21). However, in other varieties, outside London, Middle English Open Syllable Lengthening-affected *e*, *o* merged with the reflexes of Old English *ēa*, *ǣ* and *ā* > /ɔ:/ respectively. These two systems may be characterized as System I and System II respectively.

2.10 With the rise of London and the perception of there being a prestigious form of speech which coincided with it (see (a), (b), above), users of System II, whose social situation may be characterized as weakly tied, came into contact with users of System I. System I speakers distinguished phonemically between Middle English Open Syllable Lengthening-affected *e* and *o* and the reflexes of Old English *ēa*, *ǣ*, and *ā*, whereas System II speakers did not (see (c), (d) above). Moreover, it seems likely that System I speakers, with a habit of pronouncing much of their stylistically marked vocabulary in a 'French' way (see (a) above), would have distinct ways of pronouncing mid-close *ē* and *ō*; there is some evidence that French *ē*, *ō* were realized as somewhat higher in phonological space than the reflexes of English *ē*, *ō*, and this would have been encouraged by the presence of an extra phoneme in both front and back series of long vowels. R. B. Le Page has suggested that the aristocracy of the late fourteenth and fifteenth centuries were likely 'to adopt affected forms of speech as a means of "role-distancing" from the lower classes, from whom they had hitherto been differentiated by speaking French' (cited in Samuels 1972: 145–6). Finally, if the raised 'French' pronunciations of ē, ō were adopted by System I speakers, it seems likely that diph-thongal pronunciations of the close vowels ī, ū, viz. [ɪi, ʊu], which are attested variants within the phonological space of close vowels in accents with phonemic length, would have been favoured by them, in order to preserve distinctiveness. Such a development would mean that a four-height system of monophthongal long vowels would be sustained, with Middle English /i:/ being reflected as a diphthong, albeit one with a comparatively close first element.[18]

2.11 We would expect in such circumstances that hyperadapta-tions would follow; and this is the basis of the argument for the origins of the Southern Shift offered here. System II speakers, who may be characterized as weakly tied, socially aspirant incomers, encountered System I speakers whose social situation they wished to emulate.

2.12 The process, it might be plausibly argued, worked somewhat as follows. We might take the Middle English Open Syllable Length-ening-affected vowels first: System II speakers would have heard System I speakers using what they would have perceived as a mid-close vowel in words where they would use a mid-open vowel. Since final -e had been lost there would not be a grammatical rule to identify when such vowels should be used, and System II speakers, who formed the rising class of late medieval and early Tudor Lon-don, would replace their mid-open vowels (whether derived from Middle English Open Syllable Lengthening-affected e, o or from Old English ēa, ǣ, and ā) with mid-close ones. There would be phono-logical space for them to do so since they were also attempting to imitate the socially salient raised allophones of System I speakers' French-style /e:, o:/; since these pronunciations were themselves not in the phonemic inventory of System II speakers it seems likely that

---

[18] Five-height systems of monophthongal phonemes are attested in the world's languages, but are rare, and not (as far as I know) attested in varieties of English, where three- and four-height systems are much more common. See Maddieson (1984: passim).

such pronunciations were perceived as members of the phonemes / iː, uː/ and would be reproduced as such.

2.13 Such developments would seem to correlate rather well with the initiation of the Great Vowel Shift in the south. Of the remaining developments in the Shift, diphthongization of front vowels would derive from attempts by System II speakers to imitate System I speakers' [ɪi], [ʊu] allophones of /iː, uː/; such selections would be encouraged by the need to retain perceptual distance from raised /eː, oː/, which would tend to be hyperadapted by System II speakers as [iː, uː]. And, as I have suggested elsewhere, the later development whereby Middle English /aː/ > / ɛː/ probably derives from a distinct, sociolinguistically driven process. Middle English phonemic /aː/ was comparatively new in most southern English accents, being derived largely from Middle English Open Syllable Lengthening-affected /a/. The main accent in the South-East where phonemic /aː/ had existed beforehand was the Essex dialect, which seems to have been the 'old London' usage characteristic of low-prestige speakers in the area. A raised pronunciation of Middle English /aː/, probably as [æː], would have been another way of marking social distinction which System I speakers would have been keen to make. System II speakers, attempting to replace their own /aː/ with /æː/, would have tended again to overshoot, identifying the System I [æː]-pronunciation with the next phoneme in their own series, /eː/. Such a set of processes, it is held here, may be characterized as the Great Vowel Shift.

3 The Southern Shift: the Mopsae and the Easterners

3.0 The outcome of the developments just described was the distribution of vowels attested by the best writers on pronunciation in the sixteenth century. John Hart's *Orthographie* (1569) would seem to reflect a slightly modified version of System I. Hart's identification of Middle English /ɛː/ with German *ä* and French *e* (Dobson 1968: 620–1) is slightly problematic, but not so if it is accepted that his prototypical realization of Middle English /eː/

was [ẹ:] and his realization of Middle English /a:/ was [æ:]; he would have perceived reflexes of Middle English /ɛ:/ as intermediate between these sounds, but lower than System II speakers' [e:] for Middle English /ɛ:/, and an identification of his reflex of Middle English /e:/ with the French and German pronunciations cited would therefore make sense (*contra* Smith 1996: 104–5).

3.1 Eventually, of course, the system recorded by Hart died out, to be replaced by System II—which is, as we might expect given its social origins, the system found in the rhymes and puns of Shakespeare and his contemporaries (see Samuels 1972: 147; Dobson 1968: 400–1). These System II speakers, it would seem, are to be identified with the 'Mopsae', whose 'affected' pronunciation was identified by Alexander Gil in his *Logonomia Anglica* (1619, 1621). Gil characterizes the Mopsae as social climbers, weakly attached to their social class and area and thus liable to hyperadapt or overshoot when faced by linguistic systems perceived by them as prestigious. He himself favoured a pronunciation like that of Hart, with one or two archaisms which seem to be influenced by misinterpretation of spelling (see Dobson 1968: 131–55).

3.2 However, despite Gil's strictures, the pronunciation favoured by the Mopsae ultimately became dominant. By the early seventeenth century, the Mopsae would have had a system in which Middle English /i:, u:/ had diphthongized to [əɪ, əʊ], Middle English /e:, o:/ had raised to /i:, u:/ and Middle English /ɛ:, ɔ:/ had raised to /e:, o:/. Their attempt to reproduce System I's [æ:] had resulted in a merger of their reflexes of Middle English /ɛ:/ and /a:/ on /e:/; this latter development would account for their most notorious habit (according to Gil) of using '*kēpn*, and almost *kīpn*' for the word *capon* (see Dobson 1968: 145, 148). Gil plainly saw such pronunciations as affected; for him, such words had /æ:/. However, given the limitations of his own phonetic script, which essentially reflected System I, he had no symbol for the Mopsae's /e:/.

3.3 System I continued to be used into the seventeenth century, and indeed is recommended by possibly the best of the seventeenth-century phoneticians, Christopher Cooper, whose *Grammar* (1685, 1687) was cited in Chapter 2. However, there is good evidence that

Cooper's pronunciation would have been regarded as old-fashioned, and System II is thus general in the rhymes of poetry written by those English poets of the seventeenth century who represent those classes, the 'middling sort', who took part so prominently in the English Civil Wars. Edmund Waller (1606–87), for instance, rhymes *speak* : *make*, while John Dryden (1631–1700) rhymes *dream* : *shame* : *theme*; these rhymes demonstrate an identity of Middle English /ɛ:, a:, ai/ characteristic of System II. Waller and Dryden were both courtiers and prominent members of the intellectual establishment, yet their rhymes show them to have been descendants of the Mopsae. System II is also commonly attested by the 'homophone lists' which started to appear from the middle of the seventeenth century (see Dobson 1968: 400), and it was retained into the eighteenth century by writers such as Swift (1667–1745), Pope (1688–1744), and even Cowper (1731–1800), although in these cases allowance should be made for the existence of conventional eye- as opposed to ear-rhyme.

3.4 However, System II did not remain dominant, and in the eighteenth century it was replaced by a third system: System III. System III originated in East Anglia. It is attested by Gil, who refers to the speech of 'Easterners'; contact between London and the wealthy wool-producing counties of East Anglia, such as Norfolk and Suffolk, was widespread and constant throughout the medieval and Early Modern periods.[19]

3.5 Pre-Shift East Anglia had a three-height system of long vowels, viz. /i:, u:, e:, o:, a:/. One reason for the emergence of this system was inheritance from the Old English period of Anglian *ē* for Saxon *ǣ*; another reason was to do with environmentally conditioned raisings, notably when older *ǣ* was followed by /d, t, n, s, l, r/ (see further Dobson 1968: 612).

---

[19] Evidence of such contacts is provided, for instance, by the well-known *Paston Letters* from the fifteenth and sixteenth centuries; see Davis 1971–76, and also Beadle and Richmond 2006. It is interesting, and perhaps relevant to the arguments of this chapter, that several—though equally interestingly by no means all—male Pastons modified their spelling-practices to reflect usages current in London. See for instance Davis 1983.

3.6 When System III speakers came into contact with System I, hyperadapting tendencies took over. For System III speakers would tend to perceive System I [æ:] as /e:/, System I [ẹ:] as /i:/, and would consequently have a more 'advanced' diphthongal pronunciation of the reflex of Middle English /i:/, probably [əɪ]. A similar situation would hold with the back vowels. Since Middle English /e:/-words and Middle English /ɛ:/-words had merged in this dialect before the Shift, both would have been involved in the raising to /i:/, and this would account for Gil's description of the Easterners' 'thinness' of pronunciation.

3.7 During the late seventeenth and eighteenth centuries, immigration into London from the countryside continued, for the same reasons as that which impelled Dick Whittington. Plays such as Farquhar's *The Recruiting Officer* or Gay's *Beggar's Opera*, where provincials are gulled by urban semi-sophisticates, or the career of Dr Johnson, from comparative impoverishment in Lichfield to cultural iconicity in London, are manifestations of a much more common demographic process. East Anglia was a major source of such immigration, as the wool trade began to suffer from the impact of competition from alternative kinds of clothing material, and System III speakers were, as a result, more commonly part of the London speech community (see e.g. Bindoff 1950: 181 and passim.)

3.8 System III, in which Middle English /ɛ:, e:/ were reflected in /i:/ and Middle English /a:, ai/ in /e:/, had certain functional advantages, for System III allowed fewer homophonic clashes than System II (see Smith 1996: 110 and references there cited). However, the fact that System II remains, albeit modified, in many accents of English indicates that functional constraints are not alone responsible for the adoption of System III in the capital (see Wells 1982: 194ff; 'stage-Irish' *tay* for 'tea' is a System II form).

3.9 The reason seems to be simply one of availability. System II and System III could only come into competition in a major urban centre; in more rural areas the opportunity for the two systems to compete would have been much rarer and in any case constrained by the close social ties characteristic of rural communities. As I have argued elsewhere, the 'coexistence of System II and System III in one place, London, meant that it was possible for Londoners to choose between them' (Smith 1996: 110).

3.10 The Southern Shift, therefore, can be explained as the result of attested sociolinguistic processes for which there is a fair amount of contemporary evidence. However, it was not the only process of its kind within the English-speaking continuum, and it is to a similar but distinct development, the Northern Shift, that we now turn. (See Smith 2004 for an earlier Version of this discussion.)

4 The Northern Shift

4.0 The origins of the Northern Shift have not received the same attention as those of the Southern version. Traditionally, the Shift in the north has been seen as less developed simply because further away from the point of innovation: on the model of the stone dropped in the pond, the ripples are smaller the further away from the point of impact. A more developed version of this view relates to the fact that the input to the Shift in the north differed markedly from that in southern varieties. According to this view, the mid- and low-back vowels of Old English were fronted in northern varieties and were thus not available for raising when the Shift intervened. This fronting quite possibly derived from interaction between northern varieties of Old English and varieties of Old Norse (see further Samuels 1989b). According to this latter view, therefore, the pressures towards raising involved in the Shift were the same in both northern and southern varieties, but their impact was necessarily more limited in northern accents since there were fewer long vowels to be subjected to them.

4.1 In the light, though, of the argument developed in this book, this explanation of the triggering of the process seems to be insufficient. Sound changes, it has been argued, are the result of very delicate interactions between speakers, and not simply mechanical reactions to an evenly applied (by whom?) outside pressure.

4.2 There are, moreover, two difficulties for anyone attempting to see the Shift in both its Northern and Southern manifestations as a single process. First, there is some evidence that elements of the Shift, notably the raising of low front vowels, happened earlier in northern England than in the south; such arguments have been made powerfully by Paul Johnston (1997: 69–70) among others. Elsewhere I suggested that spellings such as *neen* 'none', *heem* 'home' in the Ellesmere manuscript's reproduction of the speech of the northern students in Chaucer's *Reeve's Tale* seem to be attempts to represent a post-Shift pronunciation with a pre-Shift spelling (see Smith 1995); however, alternative explanations are possible, such as adoption of *heem* from Norse and consequent hyperadaptation of *neen* on the part of the scribe (see further Horobin 2003: 57–8). Johnston seems to argue (1997: 70) for a northern origin for at least parts of the Southern Shift, though the sociolinguistic basis for a southern imitation of northern usage seems to be rather arguable. Moreover, if the Shift began in the north, and was a single process, we would expect to see it occur to its largest extent there. The opposite would appear to be the case here.

4.3 Secondly, the sociolinguistic basis for imitation of southern usages in northern England and Lowland Scotland during the late medieval and early modern periods seems to me uncertain. It is true that certain characteristically southern spellings do occur in 'art poetry' associated with the Makars (see *inter alia* Agutter 1989: 17), and it has even been suggested that the Chaucerian final -*e* found in weak singular adjectives was adopted by some Scottish writers in imitation of their literary model (Aitken 2002: 70–1, though see Bawcutt 1998: 14–15 for an opposing view). But Henryson and Dunbar, on the evidence of their rhyming practice at least, had a very different phonological structure and distribution from that current in southern England. Moreover, the Shift seems to have been well under way in northern England and Lowland Scotland long before the existence of an identifiable prestigious southern accent which was adopted much beyond the London area. The evidence is that the modification of northern English and Scottish accents in the direction of southern usage is in general a somewhat later phenomenon than the period of the Shift, probably as late as the eighteenth century (see Jones 1995, and Smith forthcoming for a discussion of some cultural implications).[20]

4.4 Further, it is worth recalling that similar outcomes in the history of sounds can often derive from diverse origins. It is thus quite possible that the Northern and Southern Shifts, though in some ways similar, could be differently triggered, a suggestion which has already been made: 'It is possible that the actual circumstances of initiation may have varied in each area' (Samuels 1972: 145 n. 3.).

4.5 The question, therefore, remains as to the actuation—as opposed to the description—of the Shift in Northern varieties of English and Scots, and a hypothesis as to the origins of this Northern Shift is offered in the remainder of this chapter. This hypothesis will be preceded by a discussion of the standard authority (Aitken 2002), during which the development in particular of four older Scots long vowels will be brought under review.

5 The Northern Shift: Aitken's discussion

5.0 A. J. Aitken's authoritative, posthumous survey of the vowels of the Older Scots period is descriptive and evidence-based, and says little about the actuation of the Shift (it emerged, he states, 'just as in [southern Middle English], and presumably by a shared impetus', 2002: 109), although Macafee, in her introduction to his study, quotes Aitken's general views on sound change as relating to socio-linguistic development (2002: xxix). Moreover, it should be noted that Aitken's study was at least in part unfinished (e.g. in his discussion of the short vowels; see 2002: 151, Editor's Comment). Nevertheless, Aitken assembles all the evidence needed for an hypothesis as to the origins of the phenomenon in northern/ Scottish usage.

---

[20] Like Bawcutt, I tend to scepticism about 'hypercorrect' use of -*e* in the verse of the Scottish Chaucerians, since even in southern England understanding of the grammatical basis for Chaucer's use of inflectional final -*e* seems to have disappeared by the middle of the fifteenth century. See further Samuels (1988). For the impact of 'Chaucerian' usage in Scotland, with special reference to spellings, see Horobin (2003).

5.1 Aitken's description of the operation of the Northern Shift is crisply stated in terms of his seminal categorization of Older Scots vocalism. Within the Older Scots period, Aitken distinguishes Early Scots (i.e. pre-Great Vowel Shift) from Middle Scots (i.e. post-Great Vowel Shift). He captures the historical relationship between phonemes by numbering. Of these, the most important for our purposes are the historic long vowels, characterized by him as follows:

Vowel 1 = Early Scots /iː/ > Middle Scots /eːi/
Vowel 2 = Early Scots /eː/ > Middle Scots /iː/
Vowel 3 = Early Scots /ɛː/
Vowel 4 = Early Scots /aː/ > Middle Scots /eː/
Vowel 5 = Early Scots /ɔː/ > Middle Scots /oː/*
Vowel 6 = Early Scots, Middle Scots /uː/
Vowel 7 = Early Scots /yː/ > Middle Scots /øː/

*I have used /ɔː/ instead of Aitken's notation /ǫ̈ː/, which seems to me overly narrow.

5.2 Aitken (2002: 73–81) gives an exhaustive listing of the sources for these vowels, which need not be repeated in full here; a few general points will suffice at this stage. Vowel 4, for instance, is above all the reflex of Old English/Old Norse /aː/, while Vowel 7 is primarily derived from Old English/Old Norse /oː/; the fronting of these two vowels, as indicated in 1.3, above, has been plausibly derived from Old English–Old Norse interaction. Open Syllable Lengthening (see ch. 5) is the primary source for Vowel 5 and Vowel 3. Vowel 6 is remarkably stable, reflecting most commonly Old English /uː/.

5.3 One major problem for the student of medieval English and Scottish vocalism is not, however, addressed straightforwardly by Aitken: the question of the range of vowel heights available. During the Old English period, it is conventional to distinguish a three-height system, but it seems likely that there was in reality a diatopically arrayed mixture of systems: some with three heights, some with four, as was seen in sections 2 and 3.

5.4 At face value, Aitken's schema would call for a four-height system for the Early Scots period (2002: 3), but closer examination shows a divergence between short- and long-vowel systems—something found in a number of varieties of Germanic (e.g. Swedish; I owe this example to Roger Lass). Aitken's inventory, therefore, may be recouched accordingly, as Figure 6.3; diphthongs are not included in this schema (though they will be discussed further below). For comparative purposes, I also include a traditionally organized Old English three-height schema. (For the quality of short vowels, not further explored here, see Chapter 5.)

5.5 In what follows, the issue of vowel heights will become important. Before turning to this issue, however, it is necessary to examine four of Aitken's long vowels in further detail and in the following order: Vowel 5, Vowel 7, Vowel 3, and Vowel 4.

6 Aitken's Vowel 5

6.0 Aitken's Vowel 5, Middle Scots /oː/, seems to stand rather apart from the history of the other Older Scots vowels. It is in a sense a

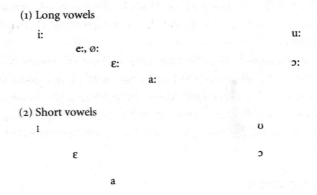

(1) Long vowels

iː				uː
	eː, øː			
		ɛː		ɔː
			aː	

(2) Short vowels

ɪ		ʊ
	ɛ	ɔ
	a	

(3) Vowel system of Old English (with traditional symbols, derived with modifications from Aitken 2002: 5, diphthongs not included)

front		back	
long	short	long	short
i, ȳ	i, y	ū	u
ē	e	ō	o
ǣ	æ	ā	a

FIGURE 6.3 The vowel inventory of Early Scots (derived with minor modifications from Aitken 2002: *passim*)

'new' vowel, since it primarily derived from an allophone of pre-Scots /ɔ/ with Open Syllable Lengthening; other sources are Old French. In southern Middle English, the vowel derived from Open Syllable Lengthening generally (though not universally) merged with the congener of Scots Vowel 4, but Vowel 4 was, of course, fronted in Scots without rounding.

6.1 It would seem neat to include the raising of Early Scots /ɔ:/ > Middle Scots /o:/ as part of the Great Vowel Shift, and indeed Aitken includes the raising in his schematization of the sound change (2002: 111). But simply because a phenomenon is like other phenomena it does not need to derive from the same process, and Aitken indeed suggests that the raising of Vowel 5 derives from a separate development: 'A half-close realisation is virtually universal for vowel 5 in [central dialects] and [southern dialects] except the [south-west]; quite likely the [fifteenth-century] smoothing of /au/ vowel 12 to [ɑ:] or [ɔ:], occupying the low back vowel slot, encouraged merger-avoiding raising of vowel 5' (2002: 87). There was of course room for such a raising since Vowel 7 had already vacated the mid-/mid-close slot in the phonological structure through a pre-Scots fronting.

6.2 The view expressed here is that this raising of Vowel 5 is a separate development, unconnected with the rest of the Northern Shift—for the simple reason that there is no need to suggest a connection other than of date; and, in order to avoid multiplying unnecessary entities, no connection need therefore be supposed.

7 Aitken's Vowel 7

7.0 Aitken's discussion of Vowel 7 (notably 2002: 39–42), characterized by him as Early Scots /y:/ > Middle Scots /ø:/ with merger between and subsequent common development of forms reflecting pre-Scots /o:/ and Old French /y:/, raises some difficulties. Aitken's view is that the fronting of Vowel 7 was preceded by a raising, leading to Early Scots /y:/ at which point the merger with Old French /y:/ took place. This account means that he has to introduce an extra lowering to Middle Scots /ø:/ to account for residual pronunciations in [ø:], with subsequent re-raisings in many Scots accents to produce a later /y:/—a further sound change which seems to have happened in time to be noted by Thomas Smith in 1542 (see Dobson 1968: 49, 701). (The fairly widespread appearance of [ø(:)]-type reflexes of Vowel 7 in areas likely to retain more old-fashioned usage, such as the comparatively rural district of Angus in the southern part of north-east Scotland, as opposed to more 'progressive' areas such as Scotland's Central Belt, suggests that [ø(:)]–type pronunciations are relicts of earlier usages.)

7.1 This is not the view of all those who have studied the process. Johnston (1997: 69), for instance, gives a different opinion, which may be regarded as the traditional view (see also, for a clear account, Lass 1984: 128):

While the likely initial value after fronting was something like the [ø:] found today in Shetlandic and Orcadian, vowel quality differed from area to area, with the north having the highest, most peripheral values, and northern English timbres apparently centring on [ʏ:] (which became [ɪʊ] in the sixteenth to nineteenth centuries).

7.2 The balance of probability seems to remain with the traditional view, whereby Vowel 7 developed originally to /ø:/, with frequent raising to /y:/ where length was retained but with sporadic shortening to [ʏ] (which may be seen as the short congener to a mid-close long vowel /ø:/, not /y:/), for the following reasons. First, it seems likely that the fronting of Vowel 7 relates to Norse; this is indicated, for instance, by its present-day geographical distribution (see various maps in Kolb 1966, e.g. p. 201). A fronting of Vowel 7 can be plausibly accounted for as part of Norse–English interaction (see Samuels 1989b); a preliminary raising cannot be so easily accounted for. Secondly, the traditional account allows a plausible space in terms of chronology for the split whereby Old French /y:/ in final and hiatical position became, in Early Scots, [y:u], which with unrounding of the first element merged with Aitken's diphthongal vowels 14a (i) and (ii), /i:u/ (see Aitken 2002: 30). Finally—and this is perhaps the strongest argument—the process as described by Aitken in 2002, which calls for a raising, followed by a fronting, followed by a lowering, and then another raising, none of which can plausibly be accounted for, seems unnecessarily complicated.

7.3 Aitken's discussion is nevertheless a stimulating one, since it raises some questions about the initiation of subsequent change, and there are also some interesting questions to do with date and spelling representation. The main evidence for Early Scots /y:/ as the direct reflex of pre-Scots /o:/ consists of rhymes with French /y:/, spelled <u>; such rhymes are early recorded in northern Middle English, for example, *fortune: sone* 'immediately' (Old English *sōna*) in the writings of the Yorkshire writer Richard Rolle (*c*.1340). Early adoption of the spelling <u> as the spelling for Vowel 7, in northern Middle English spellings from the *Lay Subsidy Rolls* (e.g. *Gudeknaue* 1296) is also indicative of an identity with French /y:/, itself represented by the spelling <u>. (These examples are given, along with others, by Aitken 2002: 40; see references there cited.)

7.4 The spelling <u> is here of interest, and would seem at first sight to support Aitken's argument against the traditional view. The adoption of <u> as the spelling for Vowel 7, rather than the simple transference of what must have been the traditional spelling <o> mapped onto a new sound-equivalent (in the manner of <i> in Present-Day English *life*, Old English *līf*), suggests that the choice of spelling (not necessarily the sound change), took place after the emergence of a 'new' Middle English and Early Scots long mid-back vowel for which <o> was an obvious spelling, viz. Aitken's Vowel 5. The spelling <u> was certainly used in varieties of Old French to represent /y/ (Pope 1934: 278). If a Scottish or northern English scribe were looking for rhymes and spellings in French to represent [ø], they were available; Old French did have a rounded front mid vowel [ø] (Pope 1934: 201), represented by spellings such as <eu, ue> (Pope 1934: 278). The sound was described fairly accurately by Louis Meigret in 1550 as '*e* close and *u*' (cited and translated Pope 1934: 212).

7.5 However, the traditional view of the fronting and raising process does not preclude an early raising following from fronting, perhaps even by the middle of the fourteenth century as suggested by Brunner (1970: 15) for example, which would allow for the mapping of <u> onto /y(:)/; and such a raising (unlike a preliminary raising of pre-Scots /o:/) can plausibly be accounted for, as we shall see; indeed, though Aitken does not implicate Vowel 7 in the Northern Shift, it is possible that it should be so included. But, before pursuing this issue further we need to address a further problem: Aitken's Vowel 3.

8 Aitken's Vowel 3

8.0 Aitken's Vowel 3, Early Scots /ɛ:/, is something of an oddity, and Aitken recognizes this by devoting a special section to its subsequent development (2002: 117–22). But before examining this subsequent development it is worth exploring in some detail its sources (Aitken 2002: 76–7). It will quickly become apparent that these sources are not straightforward, and that the evidence for Vowel 3 raises problems; but it will also be very significant for the account of the origins of the Northern Shift offered here.

8.1 Aitken identifies ten sources for Vowel 3, as follows:

(1) Pre-Scots [ɛ] with Open Syllable Lengthening (the most prolific source of tokens);
(2) Old English *ēa*;
(3) Old English *ea* +[*rd*];
(4) Old English *ǣ*(2), the result of i-Mutation;
(5) Old English *ǣ*(1) (rarely);
(6) Old French *ē*;
(7) Old French *es* in *breme* 'bream';
(8) Old French *e* in hiatus;
(9) Old French *ai* before *t, d, s, n, r,* and *g,* and countertonic *ai* and *ei* similarly;
(10) *were, weir* 'wire'.

8.2 Aitken's examination of tokens in Older Scots for these sources reveals that most have by-forms containing Vowel 2. Vowel 2 can be supposed as an alternative pronunciation for (2), (3), (4), and (5). Aitken claims that (6) has [ɛ:] in so-called 'learned words', and quotes A. J. Bliss (1969) to this effect; but Bliss perhaps offers a more nuanced account than Aitken suggests:

Words borrowed into Middle English show no peculiarities, except that the quality of long *ē* in words of this type seems to diverge from the [Old French] quality: in [Old French] this *ē* was apparently always open, except finally, when it was closed; in Middle English, on the other hand, some words have close *ē*, others open *ē*, irrespective of the context; according to Luick, early borrowings had [mid-close] *ē*, later borrowings [mid-open] *ē*, but this distinction does not seem entirely reliable. (1969: 177)

8.3 For the remaining cases, it is noticeable that almost all the examples given by Aitken have Vowel 3 in environments where raisings are pretty well attested in many late Middle English dialects, notably in the environment of following /d, t, s, n, l, r/; for details of this raising, with full references, see Dobson (1968: 635–43) and references there cited. If Dobson's discussion is accepted, 'it follows that all "Middle English [open] *ē* words" had developed, before or during the Middle English period, a variant pronunciation with Middle English [close] *ẹ̄*' (Dobson 1968: 632). Dobson considers such raisings to be 'characteristic of Northern and Eastern dialects' (1968: 635); although he uses the term 'Northern' fairly loosely, it seems likely that he includes within it the Scots-speaking area.

8.4 It therefore seems likely that Vowel 3, though undoubtedly a feature of Older Scots phonology and generally recorded in the rhyming practice of fifteenth-century poets (Aitken 2002: 119), was nevertheless in some sense unstable in comparison with other long vowels, simply because those words containing it regularly had variants with Vowel 2. This point is well made by Aitken in his discussion (2002: 117–18).

9 Aitken's Vowel 4

9.0 Vowel 4 is characterized by Aitken thus: Early Scots /aː/ > Middle Scots /eː/. The major sources for this vowel are Old English/Old Norse *ā* (i.e. /ɑː/ with subsequent fronting) and

Pre-Scots /a/ with Open Syllable Lengthening; at a later date it merged with Vowel 8 (Early Scots /ai/ in Aitken's characterization).

9.1 Aitken's outline suggests that Vowel 4 leap-frogged Vowel 3 en route to its current position. This seems unlikely; if Vowel 3 were an optional feature in Older Scots phonology, then we would expect to find a wide range of post-raising realizations for Vowel 4, either [ɛ:] or [e:]. It seems likely that the first raisings of Vowel 4 were to [ɛ:]; however, as the three-height system reasserted itself, [e:]-type realizations would have become more prototypical.

9.2 More importantly, the question arises as to the origins of this raising; for even if it was becoming common for tokens with Vowel 3 to have Vowel 2 in their place that does not necessarily mean that Vowel 4 tokens could be transferred to Vowel 3 automatically. Various reasons could be put forward for this development, and quite possibly several factors acted in combination. First, in a reconstituted three-height system where Vowel 3 was ceasing to occupy a mid-open position there would be a wide phonological space available for a variety of realizations; there would thus be room for raising to take place.

9.3 However, this can be only part of the story, and it is possible that the role of Vowel 8 may be significant in the development of Vowel 4, especially since there were many etymological doublets wherein Vowel 4 alternated with Vowel 8 (Aitken 2002: 141–2). Aitken (2002: 91) gives a wide range of sources for Vowel 8, with original pronunciations including [ei], [ɛi], and [ai]; these he considers to have fallen together on [ai] by the Early Scots period (see further Aitken 2002: 47). However, it seems likely that [ei]- and [ɛi]-type pronunciations continued to be perceived, in loan-words from Old French and Anglo-Norman, for example. From the evidence of French, there were probably even by-forms with [ɛ:] (see Bliss 1969: 175–6). Smoothings of Vowel 8, with subsequent merger with Vowel 4 in a number of environments, are also recorded by Aitken (2002: 67). In such circumstances, raised variants would have been available for selection—and may even have been favoured if 'French'-type pronunciations were preferred for stylistic reasons.

9.4 It is just possible that another source of Vowel 8, Old Norse *ei*, has implications for tokens which have been traditionally assigned to Vowel 4. Smoothing of *ei* to *ē* is recorded in a number of Norse varieties, notably Old Danish (see Haugen 1976: 210). Now, Norse cognates of 'Old English /ɑː/-words' had *ei*> *ē*, e.g. *steinn* 'stone' (Old English *stān*), *heimr* 'home' (Old English *hām*). It seems at least possible that the existence of Norse by-forms for such words would have encouraged hyperadaptations, of which raising would have been one.

9.5 In short, there was the space and the impetus for Vowel 4 to undergo raising as a distinct part of the Northern Shift. The dating is uncertain (just as is the dating of the merger of Vowels 4 and 8; see Aitken 2002: 141–5), but quite possibly is related to the phonemicization of Open Syllable Lengthening which produced Vowel 3.

10 The actuation of the Northern Shift

10.0 It is at this point that we might pose the question raised in 5.3: how many heights of long vowel did Older Scots have? The inherited Old English system, of course, was essentially a three-height system with *ī* (with *ȳ* as the rounded equivalent), *e* and *æ*: as front vowels and *ū*, *ō*, and *ā* as back vowels. Traditionally, the Northern fronting of Old English/Old Norse *ā* /ɑː/ and the Southern borrowing of Old French *ā*, accompanied by Open Syllable Lengthening of Old English *a/ae*, has been seen as producing in both dialects a new long front vowel which is henceforward characterized phonemically as /ɛː/ (i.e. Vowel 3). This process disturbed the old three-height system and produced a new four-height pattern.

10.1 Now it is reasonably clear from the history of both northern and southern varieties that four-height systems of long vowels were in some sense unstable. In the south, as we saw in Section 4, System II was subject to disturbance and replacement when System III became available. It seems also that Vowel 3 in northern varieties was similarly vulnerable, in that it seems to have been an optional item in the Older Scots phonemic inventory.

10.2 It will be recalled that it was suggested in sections 2 and 3 that triggers for the Southern Shift are to be found in the mid-vowel areas, in hyperadaptations consequent on the distinct phonemicization of lengthened vowels produced by Open Syllable Lengthening; in other words, the Southern Shift is the result of an H&H-type process of the kind discussed in earlier chapters. Although the origins of the Northern Shift are clearly distinct, is it possible to perceive the working of a similar (if distinct) process with regard to the Northern Shift?

10.3 It is argued here that a plausible hypothesis along these lines as to the actuation of the Northern Shift may be derived from the discussion presented so far. The evidence suggests that Vowel 3, a newcomer, disturbed the vowel geometry of the northern long-vowel system. What Aitken refers to as 'lexical misplacement'—derived, it might be argued, from the existence of common by-forms with Vowel 2—suggests uncertainty amongst speakers as to how to deal with the new sound. Such uncertainties have been frequently recorded during the reorganization of phonological space consequent on the appearance of new phonemes; the well-known effects of such developments have already been discussed in Chapter 3, 9.7.

10.4 It is argued here, therefore, that the Northern Shift is primarily the result of the emergence, albeit temporarily, of Vowel 3. The Shift occurred when it did because Vowel 3 emerged when it did—quite possibly not long after the loss of final -*e* and other inflexional endings in Northern dialects allowed for the phonemicization of Open Syllable Lengthening vowels in the Early Scots period. The Shift did not recur because Vowel 3 eventually disappeared from the system.

10.5 There remain of course some outstanding issues. One issue is to do with dating, and with the relative chronology of the raising and diphthongization associated with the Shift. The rhyming evidence of John Barbour's poetry, though frequently made uncertain because of his habit of rhyming stressed vowels with those which must have received less stress (e.g. *hy* 'high': *deliuerly* 'quickly'), suggests that the Northern Shift had not yet begun in

1375, the traditionally ascribed date for *The Bruce*. However, if the Northern Shift was under way by the late fourteenth century—as suggested by some rhymes in James I's *The Kingis Quair*, which dates from the beginning of the fifteenth century—then we have a rough terminus *post quem* for the emergence of at least part of the Shift. Interestingly, Aitken's analysis of the fifteenth-century rhyming evidence is as follows:

> The preceding indications that Early Scots /a:/ vowel 4 was moving towards [ɛ:] and /e:/ vowel 2 towards [i:] in the early to mid [fifteenth century], whereas /i:/ had not yet started to shift around [the late fourteenth century/ early fifteenth century], might suggest a 'push chain' rather than a 'pull chain' mechanism for [the Great Vowel Shift] in Older Scots.   (2002: 114)

10.6 This reading of the evidence would sit well with the hypothesis presented here, which might now be summarized thus. Tokens which originally had Vowel 3 began to appear with Vowel 2. In order to maintain distinctiveness, tokens with original Vowel 2 began to encroach in realization upon those with Vowel 1, which in turn began to adopt diphthongal realizations in order to maintain phonological space. Such an account sits well with the sequencing suggested by Aitken and derived from his analysis of the rhyming evidence (2002: 109–10).

10.7 In this narrative, the raising of Vowel 4 is a separate issue (the distinction between a 'higher' and 'lower' shift has been suggested before, for instance by Johnston 1997: 70 (see also references there cited) although the processes described here are rather different), though no doubt encouraged by the growing availability of phonological space in the mid-vowel region.

10.8 There remains the question of the raising of what has here been assumed to be the post-fronted value of Vowel 7, i.e. /ø:/. Since this was a rounded vowel, there would seem at first sight to be no good reason why raising is necessary to sustain phonological space.

10.9 However, it is worth noticing that, in the history of English and Scots, there is a persistent tendency of front vowels to undergo unrounding; rounding, in the phonological inventories of these varieties, is essentially a secondary feature of back vowels, and words with rounded front vowels frequently have variant congeners with unrounded front vowels (cf. present-day Glaswegian [fɪt] 'foot' beside [fʏt]). Although the evidence is slight (as would be expected in the comparatively formal written records of the fifteenth century), we can presume with some confidence the existence in Middle Scots of an /e:/-variant of Vowel 7, as indeed appears in certain Modern Scots varieties (see Aitken 2002: 41). The existence of such variants would plausibly have encouraged the adoption of raised forms of both rounded and unrounded vowels as the reflex of Vowel 1, viz. /i:, y:/. That such raising is the outcome rather than the result of the Shift is suggested by the fact that <i> spellings are occasionally found in sixteenth-century documents (Aitken 2002: 41), and by the fact that the raised but unrounded forms which are the reflex of Vowel 7 have not been subjected to the Shift themselves, as one might otherwise expect.

10.10 Although the focus of this chapter has been on the mechanical processes involved in a 'chain-shift', it is perhaps worth noticing that the Shift does correspond in dating to a major development in the history of Scots: the process of gradual elaboration which was to lead, by the beginning of the sixteenth century, to its position as a quasi-standard language, available for 'high' and 'low' registers. Such developments in English are known to have corresponded with the Southern Shift, since hyperadaptation was encouraged at times when the socially ambitious—necessarily weakly tied to the social groups they were emerging from and aspired to—were flagging their rising status by linguistic means. Hyperadaptations of the kind described can only have been encouraged by such circumstances.

10.11 No doubt many further difficulties with the hypothesis proposed here need to be addressed. But this hypothesis, it is argued, has at least some historical plausibility: that the Northern Shift is the result of the reorganization of phonological space consequent on the appearance of a new phoneme, namely, Vowel 3, and subsequent reorganizations of other front vowels. The Shift, it is held here, had nothing to do with back vowels (*pace* Aitken 2002: 111). In one sense, therefore, the development of the Northern Shift is really derived from 'a shared impetus' with the Southern Shift, in

Aitken's phrase, since it too seems to derive at least in part from mechanical developments consequent on change elsewhere in the system. However, no reference to southern 'influence' is needed to account for the development in the north, and the similarity between Northern and Southern Shifts seems essentially coincidental. Of course, later developments to do with the anglicization of Scottish accents are a different matter, and merit distinct treatment.

11 Implications of the study

11.0 One implication of the study of the vowel shifts, Southern and Northern, offered here has been raised before (see Smith 1996: 110–11): is the Great Vowel Shift (singular) a unitary phenomenon? It would seem that the triggering and implementation of the Shift differed in different parts of the country. It was not some sudden, massive movement but rather a series of very small, individual choices which interacted diachronically, diatopically and sociolinguistically, resulting in at least two distinct sets of phonological realignments. The term *Great Vowel Shift* remains a useful label but, as has been pointed out by, among others, Roger Lass (1988: 396), only in the same way as 'Industrial Revolution' is a helpful shorthand method of referring to how a series of minor technological advances ultimately brought about a major cultural change.

11.1 But, of course, there are more general implications. In the next (and final) chapter, an attempt will be made to draw some general conclusions from the three case studies offered in Chapters 4 through 6. In so doing, some of the issues raised in Chapter 1 will be revisited, not least the whole question of what is meant by explaining sound change.

7

On the Historiography of
Sound Change

1 Multiple explanations

1.0 As was indicated in Chapter 1, historians have always felt the urge to explain events; but it is important to realize that single explanations for past occurrences have been, since the Enlightenment, regarded with suspicion by serious students of history. For instance, in a magisterial survey, Donald Dudley rules out single explanations for the fall of the Western Roman Empire:

Epidemics, soil erosion, climatic change, racial degeneration, immorality (a favourite view over the centuries!), class warfare, a fall in the birth-rate, the institution of slavery... none by itself was so rampant as to cause the collapse of the West.   (1975: 291)

Alternative explanations are 'pluralist' ones, 'headed by Gibbon, who saw the answer as "the triumph of barbarism and Christianity"' (Dudley 1975: 291). Dudley goes on to cite a range of possibilities: economic collapse in the West, leading to the disappearance of a city bourgeoisie; technological fossilisation; 'barbarization' of the army and alienation between governors and governed; military weakness in the face of barbarian attack; high taxation and consequent corruption (Dudley, following J. B. Bury, cites the fifth-century historian Priscus: 'even to get a hearing a man must pay the judge and the judge's clerks'); the divisive impact of religious controversies.

1.1 All of these factors make up the context within which the Western Empire fell. But Dudley goes on to make the following point:

If even one of Theodosius' sons had been a strong personality; if Attila had not been a nomadic leader of the calibre of Genghis Khan; if there had been an Emperor of the West of the vigour of Theodosius II or Anastasius in the East; if the great attack on the Vandals in 466 had been successful...then the West might have recovered.   (1975: 293)

Dudley concludes with a quotation from *On the nature of things*, by the Roman writer Lucretius. Lucretius, who lived in the first century BC, is discussing mental illness: 'but whenever things can be so confounded and entangled, they testify that, if a cause a little stronger shall have made its way within, they must needs perish, robbed of any further life' (cited Dudley 1975: 294). Dudley would thus see the fall of the western Empire as the result of 'confounded and entangled' conditions and what he refers to as 'contingent circumstances' (1975: 293).

1.2 It will have been observed from the earlier chapters of this book that individual sound changes in the history of English have been discussed in ways which fit rather well with Dudley's historiographical approach. The intention throughout has been to put aside single, all-encompassing explanations; developments in the history of the language are seen as the result of the complex interaction of context and contingency, and the traditional divisions between 'external' and 'internal' historical approaches have been set aside (cf. McMahon 2000b: ch. 1). It has been generally accepted that historical events tend to be overdetermined, 'that is they may have several sufficient as well as necessary causes, any one of which might have been enough to trigger the event on its own' (Evans 2000: 158). And such explanations fit rather well with other branches of knowledge: 'In both pure and applied science, the principle of multiple conditioning is a commonplace' (Samuels 1972: 3).

1.3 Such explanations have been offered for all the major sound changes discussed here. The Great Vowel Shifts, for instance, have been explained in terms of social interaction and phonological inputs. The quantitative developments which span the transition from Old to Middle English were similarly accounted for by a mixture of factors: contact between English and Norse, inflectional loss, the phonetic properties of vowels and consonants. And Breaking was seen as a phenomenon brought about through a mixture of intralinguistic and extralinguistic processes.

1.4 These explanations were all, however, historical explanations, that is, partial, up for debate and refutation if better, more convincing explanations or new pieces of evidence are forthcoming. If readers of this book can find better explanations or new pieces of evidence, then that is a good thing; one of the greatest temptations in any intellectual endeavour is a to find some 'final' statement as to the truth or otherwise of an enquiry. It is to such questions that we should now turn.

2 Assessment of historical explanation

2.0 How far, though, have the historical explanations of sound change offered here been successful? To put the matter more generally, how can we assess the success of an historical explanation?

2.1 One response to such difficulties is the 'postmodern' one, cited in Chapter 1 above, which holds (or seems to hold) that there is a 'multiplicity of equally valid truths' (Evans 2000: 296). Evans (2000: 127–8) cites two postmodernist historians, Ellen Somekawa and Elizabeth Smith, as follows:

Although historians often frame their criticisms of colleagues' work in terms of evidence—sources overlooked, misplaced emphasis, inappropriate categorization—such criticisms cannot demonstrate the superiority of one interpretation or story-type over another. These debates over evidence are largely diversionary; they are carried on as if the choice and use of evidence will determine a historian's perspective rather than that the historian's perspective counts as evidence.

Is it possible to apply this formulation to historical linguistics?

2.2 A postmodern historical linguistics is conceptually possible. If no explanation for an event is much better than any other explanation, then there would seem to be two alternatives: either to make a range of claims on the basis of imagination, or to refuse to explain altogether, and 'simply' describe. (The quotes round the word 'simply' are of course intentional.)

2.3 The first of these responses might be dealt with along the lines of Richard Evans's comment on postmodernism in relation to the ethically fraught issue of Holocaust denial:

...postmodernist hyper-relativism encourages tolerance of Holocaust denial because it rejects the idea that one can tell truth from fiction and interpretation from falsification...extreme historical relativism, the idea that truth about history can never be discovered, makes it impossible to refute Holocaust deniers. (Evans 2000: 312)

(It is important to point out that Evans goes on to state: 'This does not mean that they [postmodernists] would have any truck with such notions [as Holocaust denial] themselves, something I have never claimed anywhere.')

2.4 The postmodernist challenge has nevertheless drawn attention to what has often been referred to as the 'observer's paradox', the way in which the frame of reference of the investigator constrains the enquiry. However, as I have argued elsewhere (Smith 1996: 7), and as Evans has pointed out, the answer to the postmodernist challenge is to reassert the value of traditional historiographical virtues. The observer's paradox should not be seen as disabling, but rather it places certain ethical requirements on historians: to be self-critical, to be open to other interpretations of events, and (above all) to be humble. Historians are (or should be) aware that their work is in no sense a last word on a topic but simply part of a continuing discussion in which their views may eventually come to be displaced.

2.5 The second response is more tricky, and in one sense it is undeniable. As Dudley confesses in his discussion, historical change is 'in the last resort...insoluble' (1975: 291); the interaction of circumstance and contingency is so subtle that it resists ultimate explanation, a point argued forcibly by Roger Lass in a number of publications (e.g. Lass 1980, 1987; see further McMahon 1994: 44–6 for a judicious assessment of the issue).

2.6 The argument that language change is not amenable to proper explanation is thus implied by the serious statement of a major scholar: what caused him to argue as he does? It seems to me that there are two issues here. One might be termed theological (or Lucretian), and is captured by Dudley's phrase 'in the last resort'. We might argue that things change simply because everything changes: it is in the nature of things to change, and was from the moment of creation. For the authors of the Bible, or for Homer, events were ultimately the outcome of divine intervention. For the irreligious, all changes might be seen as deriving in some way from the Big Bang.

2.7   The second issue is, I would argue, a very deep one: to do with the nature of the enterprise we call historical linguistics. Colleagues in some other branches of the humanities have sometimes said to me that the kind of work exemplified by this book seems to them 'scientific'; work in this area requires the application of certain logical techniques and grasp of, say, certain notions in physics which are foreign (they claim) to their own discipline. There would seem, therefore, to be an objective neutrality about scientific enquiry which is not shared by the humanities. But, following Suzanne Romaine (1982: *passim*), I would see this view as an expression of 'scientism', that is to say, based on a mistaken conception of what scientists actually do, and probably related to the traditional anglophone division between the arts and the sciences (see ch. 3, 4.2). It is clear that scientists, just as much as students of the humanities, are keen creators of narratives.

2.8   In an earlier book, I cited two philosophers of science, I. Prigogine and I. Stengers, and it is worth revisiting their work here (Smith 1996: 196; see also Prigogine and Stengers 1984; Halliday 1987). Prigogine and Stengers engage with 'chaos theory'—which, as they point out, is really to do with very complex orderings in, for instance, physics, and state,

A new type of order has appeared. We can speak of a new coherence, of a mechanism of 'communication' among molecules. But this type of communication can arise only in far-from-equilibrium conditions...What seems certain is that these far-from-equilibrium phenomena illustrate an essential and unexpected property of matter: physics may henceforth describe structures as adapted to outside conditions...To use somewhat anthropomorphic language: in equilibrium matter is 'blind', but in far-from-equilibrium conditions it begins to be able to 'take into account', in its way of functioning, differences in the external world . . . the analogy with social phenomena, even with history, is inescapable.   (1984: 13–14)

2.9 The passage is an important one, with many implications; but for our purposes here its interest lies in the way in which the arts–science divide is broken down. Physics and history are seen as part of the same endeavour. Moreover, the description offered has clear implications for the evolution of language.

2.10 How, then, is an historical explanation of an event to be assessed? The answer is quite a simple one: it is to do with a key requirement of scientific endeavour—falsifiability. Historians sift evidence, make judgements about plausibility, are able to admit fault if better explanations are presented or new evidence appears, in other words, meet the falsifiability requirement which was identified by Karl Popper as an essential criterion for a valid branch of scientific endeavour (for this notion applied to linguistics, see Sampson 1980: 117). Richard Evans claims as much in what was originally the final sentence of his book (which he refers to ruefully as his 'much-misunderstood concluding sentence'):

. . . I will look humbly at the past and say . . . : it really happened, and we really can, if we are very scrupulous and careful and self-critical, find out how it happened and reach some tenable though always less than final conclusions about what it all meant.   (2000: 253)

2.11 This statement would seem to offer the answer to the question of assessment of explanations of linguistic change such as those in this book. Explanations of sound change are successful if they meet certain criteria of plausibility, in the same way that all historical explanations are successful.

2.12 Thus explaining sound change is an exercise in plausible argumentation. As April McMahon puts it, 'For the moment, we may have to accept a lower-key definition of explanation at a less elevated but more commonsense level: explanation might then constitute "relief from puzzlement about some phenomenon"' (1994: 45). This formulation would seem to sit well with that offered by Richard Evans.

3 Historical linguistics and history

3.0 This book is of course not in any way the first to make this connection between historical linguistics and history. In a recent important collection of conference papers, Anne Curzan and Kimberly Emmons make the following point:

> Throughout this volume, we see an ongoing conversation at the heart of historical English linguistics: the question of evidence and historical reconstruction. Robert Fulk puts it eloquently in his discussion of the oral nature of early English vernacular texts and the possibility, if not the necessity, of creating linguistic arguments based on unavailable evidence; 'it raises', he concludes, 'profound questions about explanation in linguistics, most particularly whether the aim of historical linguistics should be to explain the data available or to analyze texts of earlier periods from a realistic historical perspective—that is, whether the primary allegiance of historical linguistics should be to linguistics or to history'. (Curzan and Emmons 2004: x; Fulk's article appears in Curzan and Emmons 2004: 305–12.)

3.1 Fulk's argument is a strong one and elegantly argued, but I am not sure myself whether a choice needs to be made. One of the great problems in Western intellectual history since the end of the Enlightenment has been the fissiparous nature of intellectual disciplines. There are of course excellent operational reasons for this: it is no longer possible for any individual human to have universal knowledge in the same way that Voltaire or Goethe or David Hume or Adam Smith did. However, operational reasons are insufficient justification for turning disciplinary boundaries into insurmountable barriers. In a small way, this book has argued that linguistics and history in historical linguistics are both important, and that the 'unfolding conversation' between them is a crucial part of the future of the discipline. The explanations offered here form a contribution to that conversation.

Appendix 1 The principal sound changes from proto-Germanic to Early Modern English

This Appendix is offered as a convenient aide-memoire for less advanced readers of this book. It should be emphasised that the Appendix skates over many controversial matters, and advanced readers will find much to quarrel with, both in terms of formulation and content. Some especially controversial issues (e.g. the status of 'palatal diphthongization') are flagged. For further details, see the Suggestions for Further Reading.

As elsewhere in this book, abbreviations are avoided. Notations and conventions are those adopted in the main text (see the list of Notations and Conventions).

Many of the sound changes listed below are discussed in the body of this book; those which have not been discussed are included here for the sake of completeness.

A stressed vowel is one which occupies the peak of a stressed syllable. Syllables may be described in terms of onsets, peaks and codas; thus, in my own accent (a variety of Southern British English) of Present-Day English, the monosyllabic word *book* has an onset /b/ <b>, a peak / ʊ / <oo> and a coda /k/ <k>.

1 From Proto-Germanic to Old English (West Saxon)

Vocalism (Stressed)

In what follows, the letters A, B, C, etc. characterizing each sound change are those used in the handy scheme adopted in Hamer (1967).

Changes in the Germanic period (i.e. before the divergence of the Germanic varieties. Not all of these features are manifested in all Germanic varieties).

A. *u* > *o*, unless /_ C [+ nasal], or /_ $ *u, i/j*, e.g. *bunden* (beside *holpen*); *gyden* (beside *god*).

B. *e* > *i* /_ C [+ nasal], or /_ $ *u, i/j*, e.g. *bindan, helpan*

C. *eu > iu /_ $ i/j.* This *iu*, the product of a vowel-harmony, survives in the very earliest Old English texts, e.g. *þīustra* in the *Corpus Glossary* (eighth/ ninth century). Subsequently *īu* became *īo*. Cf. the alternation *cīest, cēosan.*

Changes in the West Germanic and 'Ingvaeonic' periods (see Chapter 4)

D. Diphthongal changes: *ai > ā, au > ǣa* (= later *ēa, eu > ēo, iu > īo*. The last two changes take place during the Old English period, but are included here for convenience. Examples of the first two are *bān, ēage* (cf. Present-Day German *Bein* 'leg', *Auge* 'eye'; see also the Bucharest/ Petrossan ring inscription *hailag* 'holy', which seems to be Gothic from the fourth century BC, and personal names in the writings of Latin and Greek historians, as in *Radagaisus, Austrogothi*).

E. First fronting: *a > æ*, except /_ C [+ nasal], [w]. The Proto-Germanic short open back vowel *a* appears as the short open front vowel *æ* in West Saxon, except in the environment of a following nasal consonant or [w] (despite Campbell 1959: 55; see Hogg 1992); thus forms such as *dæg, glæd*, with an open front vowel, appear beside *land*, with an open back vowel. Cf. Gothic *dags*, Old Norse *dagr*. This change is sometimes known as *Anglo-Frisian Brightening*, since it is found in Old English and Frisian.

Changes in the period between the divergence of prehistoric Old English and prehistoric Old Frisian, and recorded West Saxon (i.e. the 'pre-West Saxon' period)

F. Breaking of front vowels before consonant groups. The rules are as follows: *i > io/_ h, hC, rC; e > eo/_ h, hC, rC, lh* and sometimes *lc; æ > ea/_ h, hC, rC, lC; ī > īo/_ h, hC* (but see L. below); *ǣ > ēa/_ h, hC; ē > ēo/_ h* (but this last development is only found in Anglian dialects). Examples: *feohtan* 'fight') beside (*helpan*); *eahta, earm, eald, healp, nēah.* See further Chapter 4.

G. Restoration of *a: æ > a/_ C V[+back]*, and often also /_ C C V[+ back], where CC = geminate, or *st, sk.* Examples: *dagas* (beside *dæg*), *gladost* (beside *glæd*).

H. Influence of palatal consonants. The influence of palatal consonants on following vowels operated only in West Saxon and in Old Northumbrian. In West Saxon, if the palatal consonants *g, c, sc* preceded the mid and open front vowels *e, æ* and *ǣ* a vocalically close glide developed between the consonant and the vowel, producing the diphthongs *ie, ea, ēa.* Thus *e>* *ie, œ > ea, ǣ > ēa/ g, c, sc _* (where *g, c* and *sc* are palatal consonants). Examples are *giefan* 'give', *giet* 'still' (cf. Present-Day English *yet*), *sceal* 'must' (cf. Present-Day English *shall*), *scēap* 'sheep'. This phenomenon in West Saxon is often referred to as *Palatal Diph-thongisation.* There is considerable scholarly debate about how these digraphs are mapped onto the sound-system; for a judicious outline of the controversy with bibliography to date, see Hogg 1992. It is indisputable, for instance, that <e> in *geong* is a spelling convention; if <eo> in this word were really mapped onto /e:ɔ/ then the Present-Day English form would be **yeng.*

I. i-mutation (i-umlaut). i-mutation is perhaps the most morphophonologically important of the prehistoric Old English sound changes, and its processes can be paralleled in many of the Germanic languages. The rules are as follows: V[+back] > V[+ front]/_ $ *i, j*; V [+front, + open] > V [+front, + close] /_ $ *i, j*. When /i/ or /j/ stood in the following syllable, all stressed back vowels were fronted, thus: *a > œ* (although *a* had in most cases become *œ* before the period of i-mutation), *ā > ǣ, o > oe* (a rare development), *ō > ōē, u > y, ū > ȳ*. In the same situation, open front vowels were raised, thus *œ > e*; it is also possible that *e > i*. All diphthongs became *ie, īe*; subsequently, *oe, ōē* unrounded to become *e, ē*. *i, ī, ē, ǣ* were not affected; *e* had already become *i* (see B. above). Examples are *reccan* (Proto-Germanic **rakjan*), *menn* (Proto-Germanic **manniz*), *ele* (Latin *olium*), *hǣlan* 'heal' (cf. *hāl* 'whole'), *dēman* 'deem', 'judge' (cf. *dōm* 'judgement'), *brȳcþ* third-person present singular (cf. infinitive *brūcan*), *gylden* (Proto-Germanic **guldin*), and *ieldra, fieht, smīecþ, nīehst* (cf. Old English *eald, feohtan, smēocan, nēah*).

J. Back-mutation (back umlaut): V [+ short, + front] > diphthong/_ C V [+ back]. Restricted manifestation in West Saxon, since *œ* could not appear in this position, as a result of restoration of *a* (G. above), and it only took place in West Saxon if C = labial (i.e. *p, f, w, m*) or liquid (*l, r*). The rule relevant for West Saxon therefore reads *i > io, e > eo /_ C* [+ labial or + liquid] V [+ back]. Examples: *leofaþ* (cf. *libban*), *heofon.*

K. Loss of *h* and compensatory lengthening: e.g. **feohes* genitive singular > *fēos.* If the preceding V was short, that V was lengthened to compensate for the loss of *h.* Similar processes occurred with regard to medial *rh, lh*, e.g. **feorhes > fēores*; cf. *feorh.*

L. *io, īo > eo, ēo* in West Saxon. This change was still happening in historic times, and the earliest forms of West Saxon often retain <io>-spellings.

The chronology of vocalic sound changes

The reasoning which lies behind the generally accepted chronological ordering may be briefly summarized thus. *First fronting* must precede the other changes because, where relevant, the forms produced by it are subjected to later developments. The relationship of *breaking* and *restoration of a* is determined by forms such as *slēan* (< *sleahan* with loss of *h* and 'compensatory lengthening' < *slæhan* with breaking < *slahan* with first fronting). If restoration had preceded breaking, the resulting form *slahan* would not have been subject to breaking (there is some slight evidence that breaking might have preceded restoration in Old Northumbrian, yielding historical *slā* in that dialect; see Hogg 1992: 99–100).

The chronological relationship between *breaking, palatal diphthongization* and *i-mutation* is, as Campbell (1959: 107) calls it, 'a difficult question'. That palatal diphthongization follows breaking is traditionally illustrated by forms such as *ceorl, georn* < *kerl-, *gern-; *eo* has to be the product of breaking because otherwise *ie* would have developed from an unbroken *e* to produce *cierl, *giern, and *ie* was not subjected to breaking (Campbell 1959: 108). It is now often accepted that palatal diphthongization precedes i-mutation because palatal diphthongization does not appear to take place before front vowels produced by i-mutation; the only evidence for this chronological sequence, though, is the reconstructed form *cīese* > Late West Saxon *cȳse*. As reaffirmed by Hogg (1992: 120), Late West Saxon *cȳse* 'cheese' must arise from the sequence *cȳse* < Early West Saxon *cīese* < (subjected to i-mutation) *cēasi-* < (subjected to palatal diphthongization) *cæsi-* :- (subjected to palatalization of *k-* in the environment of a preceding front vowel) < *kæsi-*; the form is a loanword into Proto-Germanic from Latin *cāseus*, and Latin/Proto-Germanic *ā* is reflected as *æ* in pre-Old English. Any other sequential ordering of forms would not yield the historically attested word.

The relationship between breaking and i-mutation is indicated by the form *ieldra* 'older'; *ie* is the i-mutation of *ea* produced by Breaking, and this would seem to confirm that Breaking precedes i-mutation.

Back-mutation must be later than i-mutation, because i-mutated forms are subjected to back-mutation, e.g. *eowu* 'ewe', derived from the sequence West Germanic *awi* > (through first fronting) *æwi* > (through i-mutation) *ewi*, with a later suffix transference of *-u* to yield *eo* through back mutation of earlier *e*; see Campbell (1959: 90). The lateness of back-mutation is attested by the fact that in the earliest surviving Anglian texts non-back-mutated forms occasionally appear, e.g. 'sitaþ' (transliterated form) on the runic Franks (Auzon) Casket, which dates from *c.* 700.

Dialectal distinctions in Old English vocalism

The following are the main dialectal distinctions in stressed vocalism in Old English, with reference to West Saxon and Old Anglian (= Old Northumbrian, Old Mercian).

1. Reflexes of Proto-Germanic *ǣ* (so-called *ǣ*(1)): West Saxon *dǣd*, Old Anglian *dēd*
2. *First Fronting*: pre-West Saxon **æld*, Old Anglian *ald*; West Saxon *bearnum*, Old Northumbrian *barnum*
3. *Breaking* and 'retraction': West Saxon *eald*, and see 2, above.
4. *Influence of palatal consonants*: West Saxon *scēap*, Old Northumbrian *scīp* (from non-West Saxon **scēp*)
5. *Smoothing*: West Saxon *weorc*, Old Anglian *werc*
6. *Back mutation*: West Saxon *witodlīce*, non-West Saxon *weotudlīce*
7. *Second Fronting*: West Saxon *dæg*: *dagas*, Old Mercian *deg*: *dægas*

Vocalism (Unstressed)

See first Hamer (1967: 23–5); see further Campbell (1959: ch. VII), Lass (1994), and (for examples from other Germanic languages) Prokosch (1939, *passim*). On Indo-European relationships, see Szemerényi (1996).

The basic lexical element in open-class Indo-European words is the *root*, which carries the primary semantic content of the word. The root is generally followed by a *theme*. Together, the root and theme make up the *stem* of a word, to which an *ending* may (or may not) be added. Thus, in the reconstructed Proto-Germanic form **stainaz* 'stone', **stain-* is the root, **-a-* is the theme, and **-z* is the ending. Roots and themes were carefully distinguished in Proto-Germanic, it seems, but in later varieties (such as Old English), many themes have disappeared or have become obscured. They are better preserved in older varieties of Indo-European, such as Latin and Greek; thus in Latin *manus* 'hand', *man-* is the root, *-u-* is the theme, and *-s* is the ending. An example of a non-vocalic theme is *-in-* in Latin *hominis*, an inflected form of *homo* 'man' (= *hom-* + *-in-* + *-is*).

Major changes

a. *ai, au* > *ǣ*, *ō* in unstressed syllables (cf. *ā*, *ēa* in stressed syllables). In Old English, these vowels appear as *e*, *a* respectively. Examples: *giefe* (dative singular), *eahta* (cf. Gothic *gibai*, *ahtau*).

b. *First Fronting*: Except in some words with low sentence-stress (e.g. *þone*), unstressed *a* > *æ* (later *e*), e.g. *tunge, ēage*, except in the environment of following nasals.

c. *Breaking*: Breaking does not take place in unstressed syllables. Rather (according to Campbell 1959: 142) *æ* is retracted to *a* (i.e. /aː/)/_ *lC, rC*, with a tendency to develop into *o*, e.g. *hlāfard, hlāford*.

d. *I-mutation*: I-mutation was fully operative in unstressed syllables, but *oe* (long and short) and *y* became *e* (long and short) and *i* in the prehistoric period, and *æ* > *e* soon after the earliest writings began to appear. Thus *e* (long and short) and *i* were the only remaining products of i-mutation, and these fell together on *e* at an early stage. Examples: *stānehte* 'stony' (cf. Old High German *-ohti*); medial *-i-* in Weak Class II verb (from *-ej-* < *-ōj-*).

Other developments

e. Early Old English loss of unstressed vowels was very frequent, in a variety of positions, e.g. *gōdne* (< *-anōn*), *hātte* (cf. Gothic *haitada*), *dæglic* (cf. Old High German *tagalīh*).

f. Early Old English shortening of unstressed long vowels: all unstressed long vowels were shortened in prehistoric Old English.

g. Parasitic vowels appear sporadically, e.g. *Lindisfarne Gospels Gloss worohton* (for *wrohton*); they also arose sporadically for syllabic *l, m, n, r*, with *i* (later *e*) after a front vowel, *u* (later *o*) after a back vowel, e.g. *Epinal–Erfurt Glosses segil-* 'sail', *thōthor* 'ball'.

h. Reduction in variety of unstressed vowels (cf. interchangeability of *-en*, *-an*, *-on* in Late Old English texts).

Consonantism

A. *Grimm's Law and Verner's Law*. *Grimm's Law* is so-called after the philologist and folklorist Jacob Grimm (1785–1863), who first gave currency to a coherent account of this sound change. Grimm showed that there was a predictable set of consonantal differences between the Germanic languages and the others of the Indo-European family, dating from the period of divergence of Proto-Germanic from other Indo-European dialects.

The effects of Grimm's Law in Old English can be seen through comparing groups of *cognates*, that is, words in different languages with a presumed common ancestor (cf. Latin *co* + *gnātus* 'born together'), e.g. Old English *fæder, fisc* corresponding to Latin *pater, piscis*; cf. Italian *padre, pesce*.

Verner's Law is so called after the philologist Karl Verner (1846–96), who accounted for some apparently anomalous deviations from Grimm's Law. Verner noticed that certain voiceless fricative consonant sounds in Proto-Germanic were realized as voiced in a voiced environment (e.g. between vowels), and when the stress was on the following rather than on the preceding syllable. A subsequent stress-shift meant that this environment was subsequently obscured.

An Old English example illustrating the process is *fæder*, with medial *d* (from earlier **ð*), as opposed to medial *θ*; cf. Proto-Indo-European **pétēr*.) Verner's Law has morphological implications in Old English; medial *-r-* in *curon* 'chose' (plural) is derived from earlier **z* ('rhotacism'); cf. infinitive *cēosan* 'choose'.

For a full discussion of Grimm's and Verner's Laws, with bibliography, see Collinge (1985: 63–76 and 203–216 respectively). See also Chapter 3.

B. *Fronting and assimilation* is an Ingvaeonic change: in both Old English and Old Frisian a distinction arose between front or palatal and velar plosives [g, k], whereby front allophones (eventually affricates and approximants) appeared before front vowels and back allophones before back. The process seems to take place after the restoration of *a* before back vowels, proven by forms such as *caru, galan*. Examples are: *cirice* 'church', *georn* 'eager'. Velar consonants however, remained not only before back vowels, but also before their umlauts, e.g. *cū:, cyning*, since the process was completed before i-mutation.

C. *Voicing and unvoicing of consonants (mainly fricatives)*: issues raised here are important for Middle English; see below.

D. *Gemination*, in various environments and at various times. VC > VCC when syncopation of vowels brought VC /_ r, l, e.g. *bettra*, Late West Saxon *blæddre* 'bladder'.

E. *Metatheses*. Cf. Old English *þrīe, þridda* beside Present-Day English 'three', 'third'. Cf. later dialectal distinctions, e.g. Southern Middle English *wordle* 'world', Southern Present-Day English non-standard *wopse* 'wasp'.

2. The transition to Middle English

Vocalism

It is traditional to refer to Middle English vowels (and indeed other sounds) as *reflexes* of the equivalent vowels in West Saxon dialect, simply because that is the dialect of Old English which is best attested. However, it is important to remember that most Middle English dialects do not descend from West Saxon.

Stressed vowels (A) Quantitative developments

a. Late Old English: *Lengthening before Homorganic Consonant Groups*, e.g. Old English *cild*, late Old English *cīld*; cf. Old English and late Old English *cildru*.

b. Late Old English: *Shortening before non-Homorganic Consonant Groups*, e.g. late Old English *cepte* < *cēpte*, cf. Old English *cēpan*; *wifman* < *wīfmann*, cf. Old English *wīf*.

c. Early Middle English: *Middle English Open Syllable Lengthening*, e.g. Old English *beran* > Middle English *bēre(n)*, Old English *macian* > Middle English *māken*, Old English *þrote* > Middle English *þrōte*, Old English *duru* > Middle English *dōr(e)*, Middle English *sōnes* (cf. Old English *sunu, suna*)

Middle English Open Syllable Lengthening: phases
Phase 1: northern (12th century); elsewhere (13th century): *a, e, o* > *ā, ē, ō*
Phase 2: Chiefly northern (late 13th century onwards), after loss of final *-e* in northern dialects; sporadically elsewhere in 14th century: *i, u* > *ē, ō*
See further Chapter 5; see also Appendix 2.

Stressed vowels (B) Qualitative developments
The reflexes of the following West Saxon vowels vary diatopically in Middle English. References to 'southern', 'western', etc. are of course very broad-brush.

a. West Saxon *y, ȳ* is reflected as <u, uy> in southern and western varieties, <e> in the south-east, and <i, y> elsewhere.

b. West Saxon *æ* is reflected as <e> in the West Midlands, <a> elsewhere (cf. *Second Fronting*).

c. The Middle English distribution of reflexes of West Saxon *ǣ* corresponds to dialectal differences in Old English. The Old English pattern was as follows:

	West Saxon	Old Anglian	Old Kentish
ǣ(1) (Proto-Germanic *ā*)	*ǣ*	*ē*	*ē*
ǣ(2) (Old English *ā* + i-mutation)	*ǣ*	*ǣ*	*ē*

Middle English reflexes of West Saxon *ǣ*, all spelt <e>:

	South-West	Midlands/North	South-East
ǣ(1)	/ɛ:/	/e:/	/e:/
ǣ(2)	/ɛ:/	/ɛ:/	/e:/

Since both *ǣ*(1) and (2) are spelled <e> in Middle English, the only way of detecting which is being used is by rhymes and from analysis of spellings in shortened forms (cf. 'Quantitative changes'), e.g. *Stratford*; *Stretford*, cf. West Saxon *strǣt*, Old Anglian *strēt*, Latin *strātus* = *ǣ*(1). Nb: In the Middle English dialect of Essex, both *ǣ*(1) and (2) are reflected in <a>.

   d. West Saxon *a* is reflected as <o>/_C[+ nasal] in West Midland dialects of Middle English.

   e. Old English *ā* was rounded to Middle English /ɔ:/ everywhere except in the North, where it was fronted /ɑ:/ > /a:/; cf. the present-day contrast between English *home* and Scots *hame*.

   f. Old English *ō* was fronted to /ø:/ in Northern dialects of Middle English; cf. Present-Day Scots *guid*.

   g. All the diphthongs of the Old English period were smoothed to monophthongs, although <eo> was retained in the West Midlands, with the probable pronunciation /ø:/. New diphthongs arose from vocalisations of Old English *w, g, h*; French loanwords supplied the inventory with the two new diphthongs ʋɪ, ɔɪ/.

Unstressed vowels

Unstressed vowel distinctions were already obscured in late Old English, as witnessed by regular interchangeability of the inflexional endings -*en*, -*on*, -*an*. During the Middle English period, many unstressed vowels disappeared (see Chapter 6).

Consonantism

A. Phonemicisation of voiced and voiceless fricatives; cf. Present-Day English *vine, fine*.

B. Loss of phonemic long consonants (cf. Old English *man* vs. *mann*).

C. Loss of *h* in *hl, hn, hr*; cf. retention of *gn-, kn-*. These developments are indicated by Present-Day English spelling; thus, for example, *lord* (Old English *hlāford*) beside *knight* (Old English *cniht*).

D. Vocalization of [f]/[l, r]_, e.g. Old English *swelgan*, Present-Day English *swallow*.

E. /w/ > ø/[s, t]_.

F. *ge- > i-, y-.*

3. The transition from Middle to Early Modern English

Vocalism

A. The short vowels of late Middle English, [ɪ, ɛ, a, ɔ, ʊ], seem to have been broadly stable in Early Modern English times. The vowel [ʌ], characteristic of southern English accents today, only emerged in some varieties as a distinct phoneme, /ʌ/, after Shakespearean times, and therefore should not be distinguished from /ʊ/. /ʌ/, of course, is still not generally found in northern English varieties of Present-Day English.

B. The Middle English long vowels however had undergone a marked change of distribution within the lexicon by Early Modern English times. This change is referred to as the *Great Vowel Shift*; see further Chapter 6. Table A1 gives the correspondences between Middle English, Early Modern English, and Present-day English pronunciation (Received Pronunciation and General American) for the reflexes of the late Middle English long vowels, plus the Present-Day English spelling of an illustrative form (which was of course established in Early Modern English times). Later developments are discussed in Chapter 6.

C. There were in Early Modern English sporadic shortenings of some late Middle English long vowels in particular contexts, especially Middle English [ɛː, oː] when followed by [d, t, θ, v, f] in monosyllabic words.

TABLE A1. Pronunciation correspondences

ME	EModE	PDE	Present-day example
[iː]	[əɪ]	[aɪ]	*life*
[eː]	[iː]	[iː]	*meet*
[ɛː]	[eː]	[iː]	*meat*
[aː]	[ɛː]	[eː]**	*name*
[uː]	[əʊ]	[aʊ]	*how, town*
[oː]	[uː]	[uː]	*mood*
[ɔː]	[oː]	[oː]**	*boat, home*

Note: ** indicates that the pronunciation given is similar to that found in present-day Scots and Scottish Standard English. ME = Middle English, EModE = Early Modern English and PDE = Present-Day English.

However, this is not a consistent process, and the modern outputs vary; cf. Present-Day English *dead* beside *mead*, *flood* beside *mood*. The variation in the present-day pronunciation of <oo> in *flood*, *good* is due to the shortening happening at different times.

D. Diphthongs in Early Modern English are a mixture of inherited forms and those which were the result of the Great Vowel Shift. A series of mergers meant that Shakespeare's system was roughly as follows:

1. [aɪ]in words such as *day*, *grey* etc. In Present-Day English, words containing this diphthong have fallen in with those containing ME [a:], e.g. *name*, but they were still distinguished in careful speech in the seventeenth century.

2. [ɔɪ, ʊɪ] had probably merged (the *joy–point* merger) on [ɔɪ] by Shakespeare's time in the speech of many, but others still kept the reflexes of the two distinct. There was also some cross-influencing between the two sets even amongst those speakers who maintained a distinction.

3. [əɪ]: the reflex of Middle English, [iː], the result of the Great Vowel Shift.

4. [aʊ] was retained in many more conservative Early Modern English accents. In Present-Day English, however, words which contained this diphthong generally have [ɔ:], e.g. *law*, *vault*, and it seems likely that this new pronunciation was already current in Shakespeare's time.

5. [ɔʊ] In Present-Day English, words which contained this diphthong generally have (in Scottish accents) [o(:)] etc., e.g. *know*, *owe*, and have thus merged with the reflexes of Middle English [ɔ:]. However, in Shakespeare's time some conservative speakers probably still retained a diphthongal pronunciation.

6. [ɛʊ, ɪʊ] had probably merged into [ɪʊ] by Shakespeare's time in words such as *lewd*, *new* etc. The present-day pronunciation with [ju] was also probably current in the speech of many folk.

7. [əʊ]: the reflex of Middle English [u:], the result of the Great Vowel Shift.

E. The vowels of unstressed syllables were [ə,ɪ]. However, the distribution of these vowels changed considerably between Middle English and Early Modern English times, since Early Modern English does not have certain inflections still maintained in Chaucerian English, e.g. the distinction between strong and weak adjectives. In the advancing pronunciation of the period, [ə,ɪ] may be generally considered to have the present-day distribution, where they are used in unstressed words (i.e. 'grammatical' words like *a, the,* or in the unstressed syllables of lexical words (e.g. *written*).

Consonantism

Consonants in Early Modern English were generally as in Middle English and, indeed, as in Present-Day English, the main differences from Middle English systems being:

1. The emergence in London English of a new phoneme, /ŋ/ in *sing*, etc.; see Chapter 3. This phoneme is of course still not phonemic in varieties of present-day northern English, although it is contextually used, e.g. [sɪŋg].

2. The loss in London English of Middle English [x]. There is some evidence for the retention of this sound in the middle of the sixteenth century, but by Shakespeare's time it was no longer used. It has left its mark on the spelling system, with *gh*; but as in Present-Day English this cluster seems either to have been silent (cf. Present-Day English *thought, slaughter, though*), or pronounced with [f] (cf. Present-Day English *draught, laughter, enough*). Some uncertainty about the distribution is indicated by Early Modern English spellings such as *dafter* 'daughter', *boft* 'bought'.

3. In Early Modern English, *r* is still pronounced wherever it was written; there are no silent Rs as in present-day Southern British English, e.g. *jar* [dʒɑ]. London English *c*.1600 was, like Present-Day General American, what is known as a 'rhotic' accent. Indeed, there is some evidence that high-status speakers continued to be rhotic in English until quite late in the nineteenth century, as witnessed by analyses carried out by scholars at the time.

4. In formal Early Modern English speech, [w, ʍ] are still kept as distinct phonemes, viz. /w, ʍ/, with minimal pairs *while, wile*. However, it seems certain that they were no longer distinct phonemes for many speakers, as indicated by Shakespeare's puns on *white, wight*. This change was not complete in standardized spoken southern English before the eighteenth century; the distinction is still retained in many accents of Present-Day Scots and Scottish English.

5. *Nation, sure, measure,* etc. are in Early Modern English, as in Middle English, still pronounced by most speakers with [sj, zj] rather than with Present-Day English [ʃ, ʒ]. However, the present-day usage must have

already been current among some speakers, since Shakespeare puns on *shooter* and *suitor* in the play *Love's Labour's Lost*.

6. Initial *w, g, k* were all pronounced in Middle English in words like Present-Day English *write, gnaw, knee*. During Shakespeare's time, these older pronunciations disappeared; this is indicated by Shakespeare's puns on *ring* and *wring, knight* and *night, knot,* and *not*.

Appendix 2   Middle English Open Syllable Lengthening of *i, u*: etymological notes

It is notable that the examples of Middle English Open Syllable Lengthening of *i, u* are restricted to northern forms, or are problematic etymologically. This would suggest that Lengthening failed in southern accents in the close series of vowels. These etymological notes on much cited forms are offered to support this argument. (See Chapter 5 for full discussion.)

Present-Day English *week* is traditionally seen as descending from Old English *wicu*, with Middle English Open Syllable Lengthening and lowering of *i* to *ē* e:/. However, there is some evidence for a form with a retained short vowel in Early Modern English; the word is paired with *wick* by Hodges in his 'near alike' list, though this may signal a common pronunciation with /i:/ (Dobson 1968: II, §10).

Early Modern English *weet* (for *wit*, verb, 'know'). <e>-forms for the verb *wit* are quite widely recorded in the *Middle English Dictionary*, but there is no clarity about length, and the evidence of later developments is that it only rarely underwent lengthening. According to the *Oxford English Dictionary*, the usage is a fairly rare, archaistic form reflecting rural usage, chiefly poetical, and it occurs in Spenser; since there is some evidence that Spenser's rural connections were with Lancashire, a northern provenance for the form would seem to be indicated.

Present-Day English *weevil* may derive from Old English *wifel*, with Middle English Open Syllable Lengthening and lowering of *i* : thus the *Oxford English Dictionary*. However, compare the *Oxford Dictionary of English Etymology* sv. 'weevil': 'Continuity with [Old English] *wifel* is not shown, and the word may be due to commercial relations with the Low Countries.' The Middle Low German form is *wevel*; if the loan were early enough, the *-e-* would simply lengthen along with other Middle English Open Syllable Lengthening-influenced *e*-types.

Present-Day English *beetle* has two chief meanings: 'beating implement' and 'coleopterous insect' (*Oxford Dictionary of English Etymology*). The first is from Old Anglian *bētel*; the second is from Old English *bitula*, related to *bītan* 'bite'. The *Oxford English Dictionary* flags some semantic overlap between the two (nb. the component 'hurting'), and it is at least possible that the two words underwent a formal merger during the Middle English period (as is indicated by the Present-Day English pattern). The *Oxford English Dictionary* also offers an alternative etymology to *bitula*, citing the form *betlas*, 'pointing to a nom[inative] *betel*, [which] has not been etymologically explained, but it may, if genuine, be the source of [Middle English] *betylle*, 16th c. *betel*, mod. *beetle*...'

Present-Day English *sweep*: The *Oxford Dictionary of English Etymology* considers this form to result either from the development of Old English **swipian*, Old Norse *svipa* or from the extension of *ē* in the preterite (Old English *swēop*); 'shortening of vowel in pt. and pp. is shown before 1400'. *The Oxford English Dictionary* (sv. 'sweep') flags some uncertainty:

[Middle English] *swepe* (taking the place of the original *SWOPE*, [Old English] *swápan, swéop, swápen*), first recorded from northern texts; of uncertain origin. Two suggestions of source have been made, both of which involve phonological difficulties. (1) The mutated stem *swp-*... This would normally have produced a mod. Eng. **sweap*, but in its transference from the northern to the southern area, *swepe* may have been assimilated to words like *slepe* ([Old English] Anglian *slépan*) to SLEEP, or *crepe* ([Old English] *créopan*) to CREEP, the process being perhaps assisted by the pa. tense *swep-e* ([Old English] *swéop*) of the original strong verb. (2) [Old Norse] *svipa* to move swiftly and suddenly. This etymology involves the assumption that [Old Norse] *i* became [Middle English] *ē*, which is not otherwise clearly authenticated, and that the intransitive sense... is the original.

Present-Day English *peel* is usually derived from Old English **peolian, **pilian*. However, the *Oxford Dictionary of English Etymology* goes on to state as follows: 'The differentiation in literary Eng[lish] between *peel* and *pil* may have been assisted by (O[ld])F[rench] *peler* peel, *piller* pillage.' A complex interchange of *e-* and *i-* type forms is recorded in the *Oxford English Dictionary*.

Present-Day English *creek* may result from lengthening and lowering of *i* in Middle English *crike* 'chink', 'nook', but equally probably derives from Middle Dutch *krēke*. The *Oxford English Dictionary* derives Present-Day English *creek* from the latter: '(2) *creke*, rare in [Middle English]..., but common in the 16th c. (whence the current "creek")...'

Present-Day English *evil*, Old English *yfel*, is commonly used to illustrate the operation of Middle English Open Syllable Lengthening: *yfel* > **ifel* > *ēuel*; *ē* subsequently raises to /iː/ through the operation of the Great Vowel

Shift. However, it is worth observing that the form *euel* may have two distinct origins depending on its geographical distribution. In the south-eastern dialects, *e* as the reflex of Old English *y* is commonplace, so there would be no need there to posit a stage **ifel* > *ēuel*. It is of course quite common in historical linguistics for the same form to emerge in different places as the result of distinct processes; we might note, for instance, the Middle English form *efter* 'after', which derives from Old Norse *eptir* in northern varieties, but from Old Mercian *efter* in the West Midlands (cf. West Saxon *æfter*).

Present-Day English *wood*, from Old English *wudu*, is problematic etymologically. Dobson (1968: II, §36, note 2) states as follows:

Wood does not show shortening of [Middle English] o: [i.e. /oː/]; its *u* (which is preserved as [ʊ] by the influence of the preceding [w]) is the normal [Middle English] vowel (? [Old English] *wudu*); but the spelling represents a late [Middle English] variant with *ō* [i.e. /oː/] by lengthening in the open syllable.

Present-Day English *door* 'shows variation because of its two-fold origin' (Dobson 1968: II, §155(b)), namely, Old English *duru*, *dor*. Blending between these two forms would allow for the Present-Day English *door* to emerge without positing the lowering of Old English *u* and the operation of Middle English Open Syllable Lengthening on the resulting *o* /o/.

Suggestions for further reading

A few suggestions for further reading may be helpful; since this is a beginners' list, I have restricted myself to books in English. On a basic level, the series *Edinburgh Textbooks on the English Language* is invaluable; the *Cambridge History of the English Language* is also essential.

The following books deal with theoretical issues of the kind confronted in this book, and may be wholeheartedly recommended: Samuels (1972), Anttila (1989), Milroy (1992), Keller (1994), McMahon (1994), Lass (1997), McMahon (2000b). Some of the broader issues are also touched upon in Smith (1996).

Blevins (2004) is a particularly exciting attempt to develop a new phonological paradigm, which seems to be congruent with the aims of this book.

For a general survey of English phonology and phonological theory, Giegerich (1992) is strongly recommended. Szemerényi (1996) includes an exhaustive survey of relevant literature. Sampson (1985) is a useful survey of writing systems.

General histories of English phonology include Jones (1989), which is interesting but maybe somewhat quirky, and Prins (1972), which is more traditional. Prokosch (1939) is still valuable. Campbell (1959) and Hogg (1992) deal with the Old English period; Jordan (1974) covers Middle English. Dobson (1968) is the standard survey for Early Modern English, though skewed towards the 'standard' accents of the period. Wells (1982), though essentially a survey of Present-Day English accents, includes a good deal of fascinating historical data.

References

Ackroyd, Peter (2000). *London: The Biography.* London: Faber.

Agutter, Alex (1989). Middle Scots as a literary language. In R. D. S. Jack (ed.), *The History of Scottish Literature I: Origins to 1600.* Aberdeen: Aberdeen University Press, 13–25.

Aitken, A. J. (1981). The Scottish Vowel-Length Rule. In Michael Benskin and M. L. Samuels (eds.), *So meny people longages and tonges: philological essays in Scots and mediaeval English presented to Angus McIntosh.* Edinburgh: the Editors, 131–57.

—— (2002). *Older Scottish Vowels.* Edinburgh: Scottish Text Society.

Allen, W. S. (1978). *Vox Latina.* Cambridge: Cambridge University Press.

Anderson, John M., and Colin Ewen (1987). *Principles of Dependency Phonology.* Cambridge: Cambridge University Press.

Anttila, Raimo (1989). *Historical and Comparative Linguistics.* Amsterdam and Philadelphia: John Benjamins.

Bammesberger, Alfred (1991). Ingvaeonic Sound Changes and the Anglo-Frisian Runes. In Alfred Bammesberger (ed.), *Old English Runes and their Continental Background.* Heidelberg: Winter, 389–408.

Baugh, Albert C., and Thomas Cable (1993). *A History of the English Language.* London: Routledge.

Bawcutt, Priscilla (ed.) (1998). *The Poems of William Dunbar.* Glasgow: Association for Scottish Literary Studies.

Beadle, Richard, and Colin Richmond (2006). *Paston Letters and Papers of the Fifteenth Century, Volume III.* Oxford: Early English Text Society.

Benskin, Michael (2004). 'Chancery Standard'. In Christian Kay, Carole Hough, and Irene Wotherspoon (eds.), *New Perspectives on English Historical Linguistics II: Lexis and Transmission.* Amsterdam and Philadelphia: John Benjamins, 1–40.

Benson, Larry D. (ed.) (1988). *The Riverside Chaucer.* Oxford: Oxford University Press.

Bindoff, S. (1950). *Tudor England.* Harmondsworth: Penguin.

Blevins, Juliette (2004). *Evolutionary Phonology.* Cambridge: Cambridge University Press.

Blevins, Juliette and Andrew Garrett (1998). The origins of consonant–vowel metathesis. *Language* 74: 508–56.

Bliss, Alan J. (1969). Vowel-Quantity in Middle English borrowings from Anglo-Norman. Reprinted in Lass (1969: 164–207).

Boersma, Paul (1998). *Functional Phonology: formalizing the interactions between articulatory and perceptual drives.* The Hague: Holland Academic Press.

Brook, G. L. (1947). *English Sound Changes.* Manchester: Manchester University Press.

Brunner, Karl (1970). *An Outline of Middle English Grammar.* Oxford: Basil Blackwell (translated by G. K. W. Johnston).

Bülbring, Karl (1902). *Altenglisches Elementarbuch I: Lautlehre.* Heidelberg: Winter.

Burchfield, Robert (1956). The language and orthography of the Ormulum MS. *Transactions of the Philological Society*: 56–87.

Bybee, Joan, and Paul Hopper (eds.) (2001). *Frequency and the emergence of linguistic structure.* Amsterdam and Philadelphia: John Benjamins.

Bynon, Theodora (1977). *Historical Linguistics.* Cambridge: Cambridge University Press.

Campbell, Alistair (1959). *Old English Grammar.* Oxford: Oxford University Press.

Catford, John (1988). *A Practical Introduction to Phonetics.* Oxford: Oxford University Press.

Cercignani, Fausto (1981). *Shakespeare's Works and Elizabethan Pronunciation.* Oxford: Oxford University Press.

Chambers, R. W., M. Foerster, and Robin Flower (intro.) (1933). *The Exeter Book of Old English Poetry.* London: Lund Humphries and Co.

Collinge, N. (1992). *The Laws of Indo-European.* Amsterdam and Philadelphia: John Benjamins.

Curzan, Anne, and Kimberly Emmons (eds.) (2004). *Studies in the History of the English Language II: Unfolding Conversations.* Berlin and New York: Mouton de Gruyter.

Daunt, Marjorie (1939). 'Old English sound changes reconsidered in relation to scribal tradition and practice.' *Transactions of the Philological Society*: 108–37.

Davis, Norman (1971–6). *Paston Letters and Papers of the Fifteenth Century,* vols. I, II. Oxford: Oxford University Press.

—— (1983). The language of two brothers in the fifteenth century. In Stanley and Gray (1983: 23–8).

Dixon, R. M. W. (1991). *A New Approach to English Grammar on Semantic Principles.* Oxford: Oxford University Press.

Dobson, Eric J. (1962). Middle English lengthening in open syllables. *Transactions of the Philological Society.* 70–124.

—— (1968). *English Pronunciation 1500–1700.* Oxford: Oxford University Press.

—— (1969). Early Modern Standard English. Reprinted in Lass (1969: 419–39).

Donegan, Patricia, and David Stampe (1979). The study of Natural Phonology. In Daniel Dinnsen (ed.), *Current Approaches to Phonological Theory.* Bloomington: Indiana University Press, 126–73.

Dudley, Donald (1975). *Roman Society.* Harmondsworth: Penguin.

Elliott, R. W. V. (1959). *Runes.* Manchester: Manchester University Press.

Erickson, Blaine (2002). On the development of English *r*. In Donka Minkova and Robert Stockwell (eds.), *Studies in the History of the English Language I: A Millenial Perspective.* Berlin and New York: Mouton de Gruyt 183–206.

Esau, Helmut (1973). The Germanic consonant shift. *Orbis* 22: 454–73.

Evans, Richard (2000). *In Defence of History.* London: Granta.

Firth, J. R. (1957). *Papers in Linguistics 1934–1951.* London: Oxford University Press.

—— (1964). *The Tongues of Men and Speech.* London: Oxford University Press.

Forster, Peter, and Colin Renfrew (eds.) (2006). *Phylogenetic methods and the prehistory of languages.* Cambridge: McDonald Institute.

Foulkes, Paul, and Gerard Docherty (eds.) (1999). *Urban Voices: accent studies in the British Isles.* London: Arnold.

Fry, Dennis (1979). *The Physics of Speech.* Cambridge: Cambridge University Press.

Fulk, Robert D. (1996). Consonant doubling and open syllable lengthening in the *Ormulum*. *Anglia* 114: 481–513.

—— (2004). Old English poetry and the alliterative revival: on Geoffrey Russom's 'The evolution of Middle English alliterative meter'. In Curzan and Emmons (2004: 305–12).

Giegerich, Heinz (1992). *English Phonology. An introduction.* Cambridge: Cambridge University Press.

Gimson, A. C. rev. Susan Ramsaran (1989). *An Introduction to the Pronunciation of English.* London: Arnold.

Gneuss, Helmut (1994). Discussion. In Laing and Williamson (1994: 58).

Gordon, E. V. (ed.) (1953). *Pearl.* Oxford: Oxford University Press.

Halliday, Michael A. K. (1987). Language and the order of nature. In Nigel Fabb and Alan Durant (eds.), *The Linguistics of Writing*. Manchester: Manchester University Press, 135–54.

Hamer, Richard (1967). *Old English Sound Changes for Beginners*. Oxford: Blackwell.

Haugen, Einar (1976). *The Scandinavian Languages*. London: Faber and Faber.

Heggarty, Paul (2006). Interdisciplinary indiscipline? Can phylogenetic methods meaningfully be applied to language data—and to dating language? In Forster and Renfrew (2006: 183–94).

Hines, John (1984). *The Scandinavian Character of Anglian England in the pre-Viking period*. Oxford: British Archaeology Reports.

Hogg, Richard (1992). *A Grammar of Old English I: Phonology*. Oxford: Blackwell.

—— Norman Blake, Roger Lass, Suzanne Romaine, Robert Burchfield, and John Algeo (eds.) (1992–2001). *The Cambridge History of the English Language*. Cambridge: Cambridge University Press.

Holmes, Richard (1974). *Shelley: The Pursuit*. London: Harper Collins.

Horobin, Simon (2003). *The Language of the Chaucer Tradition*. Woodbridge: Boydell and Brewer.

Howell, Robert B. (1991). *Old English Breaking and its Germanic Analogues*. Tübingen: Niemeyer.

Hudson, Richard (1980). *Sociolinguistics*. Cambridge: Cambridge University Press.

Hurch, Bernhard, and Richard A. Rhodes (eds.) (1996). *Natural Phonology: the state of the art*. Berlin and New York: Mouton de Gruyter.

Iyeiri, Yoko, and Margaret Connolly (eds.) (2002). *And gladly wolde he lerne and gladly teche: essays on medieval English presented to Professor Matsuji Tajima on his sixtieth birthday*. Tokyo: Kaibunsha.

Johnston, Paul (1997). Older Scots phonology and its regional variation. In Charles Jones (ed.), *The Edinburgh History of the Scots Language*. Edinburgh: Edinburgh University Press, 47–111.

Jones, Charles (1989). *A History of English Phonology*. London: Longman.

—— (ed.) (1991). *A Treatise on the Provincial Dialect of Scotland, by Sylvester Douglas*. Edinburgh: Edinburgh University Press.

—— (1995). *A Language Suppressed*. Edinburgh: John Donald.

Jones, Daniel (1956). *Pronunciation of English*. Cambridge: Cambridge University Press.

Jones, John, (ed.) (1912). *Coopers Grammatica Linguiae Anglicanae (1695)*. Halle: Niemeyer.

Jordan, Richard (1974). *Handbook of Middle English Grammar: Phonology.* The Hague and Paris: Mouton (revised and translated by Eugene J. Crook).

Kavitskaya, Darya (2002). *Compensatory Lengthening. Phonetics, Phonology, Diachrony.* New York and London: Routledge.

Keller, Rudi (1978). *The German Language.* London: Faber.

—— (1994). *On Language Change.* London: Routledge.

Keynes, Simon (1999). Adventus Saxonum. In Lapidge et al. (1999: 5–6).

Koerner, E. F. K. (1999). *Linguistic Historiography.* Amsterdam and Philadelphia: John Benjamins.

Kolb, E. (1966). *Phonological Atlas of the Northern Region.* Bern: Francke.

Koopman, Willem, Frederike van der Leek, Olga Fischer, and Roger Eaton (eds.) (1987). *Explanation and Linguistic Change.* Amsterdam and Philadelphia: John Benjamins.

Kretzschmar, William (2002). Dialectology and the history of the English language. In Donka Minkova and Robert Stockwell (eds.), *Studies in the History of the English Language: A Millennial Perspective.* Berlin and New York: Mouton de Gruyter, 79–108.

Krygier, Marcin (2004). Review of Iyeiri and Connolly 2002. Last updated 26–01–04. http://www.let.leidenuniv.nl/hsl_shl/iyeiri%20conolly.htm

Labov, William (1972). *Sociolinguistic Patterns.* Philadelphia: University of Pennsylvania Press.

Ladefoged, Peter (2001). *Vowels and Consonants. An Introduction to the Sounds of Languages.* Oxford: Blackwell.

—— and Ian Maddieson (1996). *The Sounds of the World's Languages.* Oxford: Blackwell.

Lahiri, Aditi, and Elan Dresher (1999). Open syllable lengthening in Germanic. *Language* 75: 678–719.

Laing, Margaret (ed.) (1989). *Middle English Dialectology.* Aberdeen: Aberdeen University Press.

—— and Keith Williamson (eds.) (1994). *Speaking in Our Tongues: Medieval Dialectology and Related Disciplines.* Cambridge: Brewer.

Lapidge, Michael, John Blair, Simon Keynes, and Donald Scragg (eds.) (1999). *The Blackwell Encyclopaedia of Anglo-Saxon England.* Oxford: Blackwell.

Lass, Roger (ed.) (1969). *Approaches to English Historical Linguistics: an anthology.* New York: Holt Rinehart Winston.

—— (1976). *English Phonology and Phonological Theory.* Cambridge: Cambridge University Press.

—— (1980). *On Explaining Language Change.* Cambridge: Cambridge University Press.

Lass, Roger (1983). Velar /r/ and the history of English. In M. Davenport, H. Hansen, and H. F. Nielsen (eds.), *Current Topics in English Historical Linguistics*. Odense: Odense University Press, 67–94.

—— (1984). *Phonology. An introduction to basic concepts*. Cambridge: Cambridge University Press.

—— (1987). *The Shape of English*. London: Arnold.

—— (1988). Vowel Shifts, great and otherwise: remarks on Stockwell and Minkova. In Dieter Kastovsky and Gero Bauer, with Jacek Fisiak (eds.), *Luick Revisited*. Tübingen: Narr, 395–410.

—— (1992). *Old English*. Cambridge: Cambridge University Press.

—— (1997). *Historical linguistics and language change*. Cambridge: Cambridge University Press.

Laver, John (1994). *Principles of Phonetics*. Cambridge: Cambridge University Press.

Lawson, Eleanor (1998). The 'Scottish' consonants in the speech of Glasgow schoolchildren: a sociophonetic investigation. Vacation Scholarship Report to Carnegie Trust.

—— and Jane Stuart-Smith (1999). A sociophonetic investigation of the Scottish consonants (/x/ and /hw/) in the speech of Glaswegian children. *Proceedings of the XIVth International Congress of Phonetic Sciences I*, 2541–4.

Leech, Geoffrey (1983). *Principles of Pragmatics*. London: Longman.

Lehmann, Winfred, and Yakov Malkiel (eds.) (1968). *Directions for Historical Linguistics: a symposium*. Austin: University of Texas Press.

Le Page, R. B. and A. Tabouret-Keller (1985). *Acts of Identity: Creole-based approaches to language and ethnicity*. Cambridge: Cambridge University Press.

Lieberman, Philip (1984). *The Biology and Evolution of Language*. Cambridge, Mass.: Harvard University Press.

Lindblom, Bjorn (1986). Phonetic universals in vowel systems. In John Ohala and J. Jaeger (eds.), *Experimental Phonology*. Orlando: Academic Press, 13–44.

—— (1990). Explaining phonetic variation: a sketch of the H&H theory. In William Hardcastle and Alain Marchal (eds.), *Speech Production and Speech Modelling*. Dordrecht: Kluwer, 403–39.

Luick, Karl (1964). *Historische Grammatik der englischen Sprache* Oxford: Blackwell.

Lutz, Angelika (1991). *Phonotaktisch gesteuerte Konsonantenveraenderungen in der Geschichte des Englischen*. Tübingen: Niemeyer.

McIntosh, Angus (1994). Codes and Cultures. In Laing and Williamson (1994: 135–7).

—— Michael L. Samuels, and Michael Benskin, with Margaret Laing and Keith Williamson (1986). *A Linguistic Atlas of Late Mediaeval English.* Aberdeen: Aberdeen University Press.

McMahon, April (1994). *Understanding Language Change.* Cambridge: Cambridge University Press.

—— (2000a). *Change, Chance, and Optimality.* Oxford: Oxford University Press.

—— (2000b). *Lexical Phonology and the history of English.* Cambridge: Cambridge University Press.

—— and Robert McMahon (2006). Why linguists don't do dates: evidence from Indo-European and Australian languages. In Forster and Renfrew (2006: 153–60).

MacWhinney, Brian (2001). Emergentist approaches to language. In Bybee and Hopper (2001: 449–70).

Macafee, Caroline (2002). A History of Scots to 1700. In *A Dictionary of the Older Scottish Tongue.* Oxford: Oxford University Press.

Macaulay, G. C. (ed.) (1900). *The English Works of John Gower.* London: Early English Text Society.

Machan, Timothy (2003). *English in the Middle Ages.* Oxford: Oxford University Press.

Maddieson, Ian (1984). *Patterns of Sounds.* Cambridge: Cambridge University Press.

Meillet, Antoine (1937). *Introduction à l'étude des langues indoeuropéenes.* Paris: Hachette.

—— (1967). *The Indo-European Dialects.* Tuscaloosa: University of Alabama Press (translated by Samuel N. Rosenberg).

Milroy, James (1992). *Linguistic Variation and Change.* Oxford: Blackwell.

—— and Lesley Milroy (1985). Linguistic change, social network and speaker innovation. *Journal of Linguistics* 21: 339–84.

Minkova, Donka (1982). The environment for open syllable lengthening in Middle English. *Folia Linguistica Historica* 3: 29–58.

Motion, Andrew (1997). *John Keats.* London: Faber.

Moulton, W. G. (1962). Dialect geography and the concept of phonological space. *Word* 18: 23–32.

Mugglestone, Lynda (1991). The fallacy of the Cockney rhyme: from Keats and earlier to Auden. *Review of English Studies* n.s. 42: 57–66.

Myres, J. N. L. (1986). *The English Settlements* (*The Oxford History of England,* Volume 1B). Oxford: Oxford University Press.

Nedoma, Robert (1995). *Die Inschrift auf dem Helm B von Negau.* Vienna: Fassbaender.

Nielsen, Hans Frede (1989). *The Germanic Languages: origins and early dialectal interrelations*. Tuscaloosa: University of Alabama Press.

—— (2002). The Old English Sound System from a North-Sea Germanic Perspective. In Iyeiri and Connolly (2002: 17–38).

Ogura, Mieko (1987). *Historical English Phonology: a lexical perspective*. Tokyo: Kenkyusha.

—— (1990). *Dynamic Dialectology: a study of language in time and space*. Tokyo: Kenkyusha.

Ohala, John (1993). The phonetics of sound change. In Charles Jones (ed.), *Historical Linguistics: problems and perspectives*. London: Longman, 237–78.

Page, Ray I. (1973). *An Introduction to English Runes*. London: Methuen.

Parkes, Malcolm B. (1983). On the presumed date and possible origin of the manuscript of the 'Ormulum'. Oxford, Bodleian Library, MS Junius 1. In Stanley and Gray (1983: 115–27).

Penzl, Herbert (1969). The phonemic split of Germanic *k* in Old English. Reprinted in Lass (1969: 97–107).

Phillips, Betty (1992). Open syllable lengthening and the 'Ormulum'. *Word* 60: 320–42.

Pinker, Steven (1994). *The Language Instinct*. Harmondsworth: Penguin.

Pisoni, D. B. (1997). Some thoughts on 'normalization' in speech perception. In K. Johnson and J. W. Mullenix (eds.), *Talker Variability in Speech Processing*. San Diego: Academic Press, 9–32.

Pope, Mildred K. (1934). *From Latin to Modern French*. Manchester: Manchester University Press.

Postal, Paul (1968). *Aspects of Phonological Theory*. New York: Harper and Row.

Prigogine, I. and I. Stengers (1984). *Order out of Chaos*. London: Heinemann.

Prins, A. A. (1974). *A History of English Phonemes*. Leiden: Leiden University Press.

Prokosch, Eduard (1939). *A Comparative Germanic Grammar*. Philadelphia: The Linguistic Society of America.

Raphael, L. J. (1972). Preceding vowel duration as a cue to the perception of the voicing characteristic of word final consonants in American English. *Journal of the Acoustical Society of America* 51: 1293–1303.

Ritt, Nikolaus (1994). *Quantity adjustment. Vowel lengthening and shortening in Early Middle English*. Cambridge: Cambridge University Press.

Romaine, Suzanne (1982). *Sociohistorical Linguistics*. Cambridge: Cambridge University Press.

Rösel, Ludwig (1962). *Die Gliederung der germanischen Sprachen nach dem Zeugnis ihrer Flexionsformen.* Nuremberg: Erlanger Beiträge zur Sprach- und Kunstwissenschaft.

Russ, Charles (1978). *Historical German Phonology and Morphology.* Oxford: Oxford University Press.

Sampson, Geoffrey (1980). *Schools of Linguistics.* London: Hutchinson.

—— (1985). *Writing Systems.* London: Hutchinson.

—— (2005). *The 'Language Instinct' Debate.* London: Continuum.

Samuels, Michael L. (1952). The Study of Old English Phonology. *Transactions of the Philological Society,* 15–47.

—— (1971). Kent and the Low Countries: some linguistic evidence. In A. J. Aitken, Angus McIntosh, and Hermann Palsson (eds.), *Edinburgh Studies in English and Scots.* London: Longman, 3–19.

—— (1972). *Linguistic Evolution, with special reference to English.* Cambridge: Cambridge University Press.

—— (1988). Chaucerian final '-e'. In Jeremy J. Smith (ed.), *The English of Chaucer and his contemporaries.* Aberdeen: Aberdeen University Press, 7–12.

—— (1989a). Some applications of Middle English dialectology. Reprinted in Laing (1989: 64–80).

—— (1989b). The Great Scandinavian Belt. Reprinted in Laing (1989: 106–15).

Sichel, Walter (ed.) (1910). *The Glenbervie Journals.* London: Constable.

Singh, Rajendra (1996). Natural Phono(morpho)logy: a view from the outside. In Hurch and Rhodes (1996: 1–39).

Simms-Williams, Patrick (1990). Dating the transition to Neo-Brittonic: phonology and history, 400–600. In Bammesberger (1991: 217–61).

Smith, Jeremy J. (1995). The Great Vowel Shift in the north of England, and some spellings in manuscripts of Chaucer's *Reeve's Tale. Neuphilologische Mitteilungen* 95: 433–7.

—— (1996). *An Historical Study of English.* London: Routledge.

—— (2002). The origins of Old English Breaking. In Iyeiri and Connolly (2002: 39–50).

—— (2004). Phonological Space and the Actuation of the Great Vowel Shift in Scotland and Northern England. In Marina Dossena and Roger Lass (eds.), *Methods and Data in English Historical Dialectology.* Bern: Lang, 309–28.

—— (2006). From Middle to Early Modern English. In Lynda Mugglestone (ed.), *The Oxford History of English.* Oxford: Oxford University Press, 120–46.

—— (forthcoming). 'Copia verborum: the linguistic choices of Robert Burns.' *Review of English Studies.*

Stanley, Eric (ed.) (1972). *The Owl and the Nightingale.* Manchester: Manchester University Press.

—— (2002). Old English *Þaet deofol, se deofol* or Just *deofol.* In Iyeiri and Connolly (2002: 51–71).

—— and Douglas Gray (eds.) (1983). *Five Hundred Years of Words and Sounds: A Festschrift for Eric Dobson.* Cambridge: Brewer.

Stuart-Smith, Jane (1999). Glasgow: accent and voice quality. In Foulkes and Docherty (1999: 203–22).

—— (2004). *Phonetics and Philology.* Oxford: Oxford University Press.

Szemerényi, Oswald (1996). *An Introduction to Indo-European Linguistics.* Oxford: Oxford University Press.

Taylor, John (1996). *Linguistic Categorization.* Oxford: Oxford University Press.

Thompson, E. A. (1965). *The Early Germans.* Oxford: Oxford University Press.

Townend, Matthew (2002). *Language and History in Viking Age England.* Turnhout: Brepols.

Trudgill, Peter (1999). Norwich: endogenous and exogenous linguistic change. In Foulkes and Docherty (1999: 124–40).

Upton, Clive, David Parry, and J. D. A. Widdowson (1994). *Survey of English Dialects: The Dictionary and Grammar.* London: Routledge.

Wang, William S.-Y. (1969). Competing changes as a cause of residue. *Language* 45: 9–25.

Weinreich, Uriel, William Labov, and Marvin Herzog (1968). Empirical foundations for a theory of language change. In Lehmann and Malkiel (1968: 95–195).

Wells, John (1982). *Accents of English.* Cambridge: Cambridge University Press.

Whatmough, Joshua (1937). *The Foundations of Roman Italy.* London: Methuen.

White, David (2004). Why we should not believe in short diphthongs. In Curzan and Emmons (2004: 57–84).

Wilson, David (1981). *The Anglo-Saxons.* Hardmondsworth: Penguin.

Wyld, Henry C. (1927). *A Short History of English.* London: Murray.

—— (1936). *A History of Modern Colloquial English.* Oxford: Blackwell.

Yorke, B. A. E. (1999). Settlement, Anglo-Saxon. In Lapidge *et al.* (1999: 415–16).

Zupitza, Julius (1880). *Ælfrics Grammatik und Glossar.* Berlin: Weidmannsche Buchhandlung.

Index

WITHDRAWN
SHORT LOAN COLLECTION